£2 9/25

Hunters of the Plains

Also in this series

ORANG UTANG
Monica Borner with Bernard Stonehouse

John Pearson

Hunters of the Plains

W H Allen & Co Ltd, London
A Howard & Wyndham Company
1979

Copyright © Survival Anglia Limited, 1979

This book or parts thereof may not be reproduced
without permission in writing.

Filmset in 11/13 point Plantin
Printed and bound in Great Britain
by W & J Mackay Limited, Chatham

for the Publisher, W H Allen & Co Ltd,
44 Hill Street, London W1X 8LB

ISBN 0 491 022 883

Contents

		page
	Foreword by Colin Willock	ix
	Author's Note	xii
1	How I Became a Wildlife Photographer	1
2	On Safari	14
3	My Approach to Filming	26
4	The Search for the Right Pack	35
5	Mishaps and Maasai	47
6	Kali's Litter	75
7	Conservation and Violet Mary	93
8	A Film-maker's Diary	106
9	The Hyena	121
10	The Lion	134
11	The Tokitok Ten	156
	Epilogue by Colin Willock	166
	Index	169

Illustrations

Black and White
(between pages 32 and 33)
The most effective hunting unit
'I had to find the ideal pride to concentrate on'
Many of the kills in the Ngorongoro Crater are made by hyena
Hyena live in organised clans

(between pages 96 and 97)
Mixed herds in the Serengeti
A new born wildebeest
The moment of photographic truth
Hunting dog puppies

(between pages 128 and 129)
Yearling wildebeest caught at both ends by the dogs
A tussle over food
A jackal
John Pearson with Rebecca

Colour
(between pages 64 and 65)
Violet Mary
Violet Mary on a Thomson's gazelle kill
A cheetah with cubs
Zebra are particularly wary of lion

Illustrations

MAPS
Page 48
The Six Known Packs of Hunting Dogs of Serengeti and Ngorongoro
Page 137
The Six Resident Prides of Lion of the Ngorongoro Crater

Foreword

I first met John Pearson in Nairobi in 1962. John was then flying DC3s on internal routes for East African Airways. He had made, in his spare time, two excellent bird films which East African was using to promote tourism. I recall vividly that we sat and talked on the verandah of the Norfolk Hotel and that John fired my enthusiasm about Lake Magadi, the soda lake in the Rift Valley where a million flamingo were to nest 2 years later with disastrous results. But by then, John was filming for *Survival* at Lake Magadi.

That was the start of our personal friendship as well as a relationship with *Survival*. John continued to fly for East African, shooting wildlife film in his off-duty time. After the DC3's retired from East African's internal routes, he captained Fokker Friendships. Next he graduated to international routes as a skipper of East African's then new Comets.

Much as John loved flying and particularly flying light aircraft, it became very clear where his heart increasingly lay – in wildlife filming. Eventually, in 1968 he gave up flying big jets in order to become a member of that rarest and most specialist breed of people, a wildlife, or naturalist, cameraman. There are perhaps a dozen top-liners in this world and John definitely belonged in this select company.

He preferred, I think, to freelance though this is a tough path to follow. He worked with *Survival* on a number of occasions,

Foreword

including going to Ethiopia. We were both part of a safari to Lake Rudolf (now christened Lake Turkana), which included Prince Philip in the party. Together we survived the humours and rigours of that expedition.

Soon afterwards, John and his second wife Jenny, whom he had met as an airhostess, moved to the Serengeti, where they made an excellent *Survival* film called *Serengeti Has Not Died*. They were operating in much the same territory as that in which this book is set.

We again teamed up for a film about Dr Colin Pennycuick who was studying the soaring habits of vultures in a motorized glider, jointly financed by Dr Bernhard Grzimek, the Frankfurt Zoological Society and *Survival*. With his love and knowledge of areoplanes and flight, John was the obvious man for the camera on this job. A film called *Wings Over The Rift* was the result. He refers to an incident early on in his book in which he had to persuade Egyptian vultures to crack ostrich eggs with stones. Well, that episode was for this film.

And so I come to the present time. In 1977, *Survival* commissioned John to shoot a one hour 'Special' on the hunting animals of the African plains and their prey. Not only that – as his book recounts – he was asked to shoot material for three half-hours in parallel with the major epic. The films were to be about cheetah, hunting dogs, and an area of the plains which he called 'The Eternal Triangle'.

John had taken on another enterprise. I put him in touch with Peter Grose, my own literary agent. I had always known John to be a prolific natural writer. His letters, which seldom shrank from criticism of those back at base, including myself, were never less than highly readable. They were full of theories about ecology and wildlife, some of which, as he confessed, were strictly his own. Naturally I did not agree with all of them, and nor did he always agree with what I did with his material, but most of his ideas about wildlife struck me as at least as sound as those of many of the scientists in the field. Encouraged

Foreword

by Peter Grose, John had decided to write a book. The book was to be called *Hunters of the Plains*, the final title of the *Survival* Special we were jointly making for television audiences not only in Britain but all over the world, including the 40 million viewers who watch the NBC network in the United States.

On 3 March 1978, in the Ngorongoro Crater in Tanzania, John was tragically and accidentally shot dead at the age of fifty. At the time, only half the manuscript for *Hunters of the Plains* existed. When Jenny Pearson returned to Britain in April, she brought with her a small suitcase full of John's notes which, it seems, he wrote up in the field while waiting for action to take place before his cameras and which he transcribed and typed at great length in camp at night.

All I have done is to take those notes, edit them where necessary and arrange them in a form of which I think he would have approved, to complete his book. I say 'complete', though that can never be quite true since he died before the last word had been written and the last frame of film shot for *Hunters*. Nevertheless he had finished at least 98 per cent of both tasks.

The result is, I believe, a vivid and moving account of a man living a chosen life, far outside the normal experience, and living it to the full.

Colin Willock

Author's Note

Many skills are involved in the production of any film. Some of these are more important than others. Where the cameraman sits on the ladder depends on what sort of film you are talking about.

In so far as wildlife documentaries are concerned, the cameraman is no more than one of a team. But the nature of the work involved means that he, more than anyone else, is out there in contact with the action.

Others, technically more proficient or more talented artistically, make their contributions under less enivable circumstances. But, unfortunately, while working in a cutting room or a processing lab may be the stuff that films are made of it is not, regettably, what books are written about.

So, in telling of my experiences while we were making this film, I lay no claim to greater importance . . . just greater good fortune, that's all.

J. M. Pearson
Ndutu 1977

I
How I Became a Wildlife Photographer

In March 1977 I signed a contract with Survival Anglia Limited to film for them a one-hour television special entitled *Hunters of the Plains*. Prior to this I had shot two programmes on predators – one on wild dogs and the other on cheetah – and it struck me then that a somewhat longer film, featuring the two species together, might make a rather better story than had been the case when I tackled them separately. All predators face the same problem; how to catch something that doesn't want to be caught; and here were two of them living virtually side by side in the same habitat, yet solving the same problem in two quite different ways.

I discussed the idea with Colin Willock of *Survival* who liked it. But *Survival* felt that the programme would be greatly improved if it was extended to the other main predators. And so, rather to my regret, lion and hyena were added.

The majority of television programmes run for half an hour. Actually, a half-hour programme doesn't usually last for more than about 24 minutes. The rest of the time is taken by advertisements, station announcements and so forth. *Hunters of the Plains*, on the other hand, was to be what is known as a 'Special'. Specials run for 52 minutes. But as the name implies, a Special has to be something 'out of the ordinary'. It can't simply be twice as long as a half-hour. The idea of the extra length is to allow one to deal with the subject more fully; to give the audience a detailed account of what, in this case, the hunters of the plains are all about.

So it was that I set out in search of the hunters. This book is not exclusively about the animals themselves, although obviously they play a large part. I am no biologist. Nor is it a comprehensive account of predatory behaviour as a whole, such as might be written nowadays by a 'wildlife expert', for assuredly I am no expert. To be an expert you need to live, not on the plains of Africa amongst the animals, but in London or New York within easy reach of a good reference library. No, this is not that sort of book at all. It is about the things I saw while I was making the film and what I felt about them; about the problems that arose and how we solved them. It is, I suppose you could say, no more than a personal account of my journey through a world which within a very short time may well have disappeared altogether, and I leave you to judge for yourself if this is where it's strength or it's weakness lies.

I had better start by explaining why I am in this strange, often lonely, but usually rewarding world of wildlife and wildlife filming at all. How in fact did I become a wildlife photographer. To begin with, let me say what I am *not*. I am not a camera fanatic. I do not want to give the impression that I am not interested in photography. That would be too much of a simplification. Nevertheless, I have to confess that it is the end-product that concerns me most; the photograph rather than the mechanics of producing it.

Of course, any photographer worth his salt has to know enough about his equipment and the materials he uses in order to get the most out of them. But there is a danger, or so I believe, in getting too entangled in technicalities for their own sake. What you should really get involved in is your subject, not your camera.

A lot of people criticize photographers, with some justification too. All that far too many of them ever do is to press the button and record on a strip of film whatever happens to be going on in front of the lens at a particular moment. There it is, beautifully exposed, sharply focussed, neatly composed, and as dead and lifeless as yesterday's lion kill. A good photograph should have something else. Some thing, if you like, of the photographer himself. It must add up to something more than the sum of it's technical ingredients. But it can only do this if it is an extension, not just of his eyes, but also of his brain; an expression of his love not for himself, as happens at times, but for life itself.

It is not easy, in a book, to write about the visual images created in a film. You can hang a still photograph on the wall and look at it and know that, good or bad, it has an existence of it's own. You cannot say the same about a movie shot. Each shot only has some meaning in relation to the shots that go before and after and cannot fairly be judged unless also considered in the context of voice or music or the sound effects intended ultimately to accompany it.

To lift his work above the level of mere technical competence, the photographer must be prepared to put something of himself into the picture. If he puts in enough then what comes out is a recognizable style. Not in every picture of course, but enough times to make it's presence more than just coincidence. That doesn't mean that I am knocking opportunism. Far from it. The pack is off and running and something happens – amusing, tragic, dramatic or whatever – and you manage to record it and as such it has some value in itself. And why not? A picture that shows some aspect of behaviour which would have been impossible to perceive by any other means has great value and, up to a point, it is the essence of wildlife photography. I have to confess though, that I'm not very good at *cinéma verité*.

This has a lot to do with my character. I am a rather deliberate individual, slow, in many respects, to adapt to a rapidly changing situation. The original boy on the burning deck. It is one of my limitations, I'm afraid, so I have to work a different way.

I used to be a professional pilot, flying for East African Airways. Not long before I gave up flying, largely because I had long become engrossed in wildlife filming, I suddenly realized that I had virtually no pictures of aeroplanes at all and that it was now or never if I wanted to get anything really worthwhile. If you wear a uniform you can go almost anywhere unchallenged in an airport. If, in addition, you have four gold bars on your sleeve and a set of wings as well, few people look twice at what you are doing and anyone who does so is apt to approach you with caution. Without such badges of rank, your chances of getting into a position from which you'll manage to photograph something out of the ordinary are extremely slight.

As captain of an aircraft, leaving Nairobi Airport, after you've cleared the parking area you turn right for Runway Zero Six and roll on down a long taxi-way to the take-off point, passing the fire station and the Kenya Airways base area on your right, and heading out into what appears to be bush. On the flight deck the first officer is reading through the check list and the long litany of question and answer passes back and forth between the crew. Air traffic control clearance comes in and is read back. Take-off speeds are passed up by the navigator. Just ahead of you now are two left-hand turns onto the runway, right angles to be negotiated with care since you are so far ahead of the main wheels up there in the nose that you could easily run one set of bogeys off the tarmac and get bogged down in the soft earth on either side.

When you are through these chores, you are on your way. This is where it's all happening and so this, when I made up my mind that I needed those pictures, was where I decided I would have to go.

In photography, as in most spheres of activity, it helps to know what one is trying to achieve before taking shots. My purpose was not to take lyrical pictures of aircraft as such. Few modern aircraft are particularly beautiful. What flying is all about isn't grace or artistry, or anything of that sort, but brute force and power, and the ironmongery needed to produce this is strictly functional. I wanted to try and show what it is that has to be controlled by the crew, carefully channelled into a useable form, and dominated by human beings.

While I was still standing there, figuratively scratching my head as to how to capture this on film, all of a sudden there it was, shuddering and rumbling it's way through the turn in the squat, the solid shape of a Boeing 720B bound for Addis Ababa, the Lion of Judah crouched on it's flanks, the air behind it throbbing and drumming at the ears as it went by. This was what I had wanted. The angle, the long focus lens, the jumping, blurring heat-haze made the Boeing into the brute image I had sought.

In photography, luck of course, always plays a big part and let no one tell you otherwise. Personally I have very mixed feelings about luck. All too often bad luck is synonymous with bad management. Good luck, on the other hand, is something quite different. Good fortune is something everyone needs their fair share of and photographers more than most. No matter how well organized you are, how patient, how hard-working, unless you have that little extra something going for you, you are apt to be struggling for results.

For example, I was working taking stills of vultures. There was this griffon vulture. I could see him up there through the view-finder, coming on down quite steadily, rocking slightly in the turbulence, feet extended, now slipping off a little height, turning into the wind and slowing rapidly as he dropped into the last 50 feet of his run, beginning to brake for a landing.

I'd picked him up a fair way out and was following him in, not bothering too much about focussing at first but concentrating on anticipating the exposure I'd need to get some detail into the features in spite of the bright background of the sky. I was reducing the offset of the meter as more and more of the bird began to fill the frame when he turned into his final approach.

Looking at the contacts now I can see that I gave him 3 shots in that last turn, although I had no recollection of having done so afterwards. What I can remember was holding my breath, trying to go smoothly with him, keeping him in position in the frame because he was too close for me to do much with the picture by cropping afterwards if I didn't get it right at the start, and having the feeling even then it was a good one. I had the same feeling with that other bird, that Boeing 720.

It's an odd feeling that – physical almost. In the days when I used to earn my living as a pilot I'd sometimes get it a second or so before a really smooth landing. The nose would be way up in the air, throttles closed and the stall warning just beginning to chatter and then, without doing anything more, suddenly the whole aircraft seemed to be running on cream and you could tell it was going to be, as they say, 'a real greaser'.

Now the point I'm trying to make is this. Although you'd settle into a nice steady approach, the cockpit properly organized, speeds right, and with everything just so, it still wouldn't turn out to be anything more than just a good landing ... without luck.

It was the same with this picture.

The bird is about where he ought to be in the frame. There's just enough blurring of the leading edge to show that he's alive and going and not just suspended there on wires and yet not enough to prevent you from seeing that individual feathers are starting to break away from the smooth contour of the wings and the bird is about to stall. Yet with all these things right, the picture, even though it was 99 per cent perfect, could still have been 100 per cent wrong if the eye hadn't been sharp. That's what makes it. And while you can account for the rest of it in terms of experience, the right film, the right lens – all the other factors involved – there's no denying that the eye was lucky and without a little of that thrown in at the right time, life would certainly be a lot harder for most of us.

How I became a Wildlife Photographer

Another question I get asked is 'What are you most interested in, wildlife or photography?' It's not so simple to answer as it might seem. Of course I am interested in both aspects of the business. After all, as a wildlife photographer it is natural that I should be. But it is an interest that balances out in some rather odd ways.

When I first arrived in East Africa, I was mildly interested in photography and had had a still-camera for many years. But although I did actually own a ciné camera, an 8mm. Bell and Howell, I hadn't at the time I stepped off the aircraft, ever run so much as a foot of film through it. It was brand new and still in its box.

I was also interested in natural history. At school I'd even joined the Natural History Society which, for me, was a pretty drastic step to take since I hardly ever joined anything. But the activities of the society were mainly confined to climbing trees and looking for bird's nests, and since I didn't like climbing trees (and still don't) and my attitude towards birds' eggs was somewhat less than enthusiastic, if anything the NHS served to dampen my keeness rather than enhance it.

So you could say that I went out to Kenya with a mild interest in photography and about as much knowledge of the wildlife there as the man who wrote on the map 'Here there be Dragons'. At that time, in 1954, the Mau Mau Emergency was at its height and the tourist industry, as such, simply didn't exist. There were no tourists and the day of cheap charters and the package tour was still a long way off.

If you wanted to see the animals you had to own a suitable vehicle and make your own arrangements. That wasn't easy as far as I was concerned since the vagaries of the flying roster seldom allowed one to plan more than 48 hours ahead with any degree of certainty. In addition I had exams to pass. I had joined the airline with a Commercial Pilot's Licence and an instrument rating for which I received, as a second officer, £850 per annum. This, together with my overseas allowance, brought my annual pay up to a little over £1,000. So in my spare time I set about working for my Airline Transport Pilot's Licence. In addition to the flying I was called upon to do, this left me with little time for anything else.

Even the few visits I did make to the game parks were not particularly encouraging. I simply didn't see anything. It was the flying, I think, that really aroused my interest in wildlife. We used to go to some fascinating places. In Western Uganda we had a route that took us from Entebbe to three airstrips: Kamwenge, Kasese and Kasenyi. At Kamwenge we off-loaded stores for the western extension of the Uganda Railway which had not, at that stage, reached its destination. After that there was a 10 minute hop to Kasese, an airstrip which served a copper mine up in the Ruwenzoris – the Mountains of the Moon. Since it wasn't worth climbing up for such a short leg we used to chug across in our DC3s at a few hundred feet gazing down at an incredible tangle of forest and swamp, threaded with water courses and thick with hippo. Then we were over the plains, alive with elephant and buffalo.

Kasese itself fulfilled my utmost dreams of Africa. The great golden sweep of grassland rolled on up into the foothills until it disappeared into the cloud that seemed perpetually present on the high mountain range. At one end of the strip was a small mud and wattle hut, used by the crew of an Anson, I think it was, who were attempting an aerial survey of the Ruwenzoris. We always used to walk across but there was never anyone there. Instead, inside on the table, littered with the crew's belongings, was a sign scrawled out on a piece of card. All it said was: 'It's in the fridge. Help yourself.'

There were animals all around, but they've gone now. They went with the coming of the railway. I'm not one of those people whose feelings for animals amounts to a mania which says that wildlife should come before progress, whatever that is. But Kasese was so beautiful once, only a very, very few years ago, and now it's so awful that wild dogs wouldn't drag me back.

How I became a Wildlife Photographer

From Kasese to Kasenyi was such a short distance that the more realistic captains didn't even bother to raise the landing gear. We used to stay there the night, arriving late in the afternoon, loading with frozen fish and departing again at 'sparrow's' the next day. Sometimes we stayed at Mweya Lodge in the Queen Elizabeth (now Ruwenzori) National Park. The drive there, if we were at all late, took us through the park after dark, with frequent halts and detours around the jay-walking hippo along the track who'd come out of the Kazinga channel for their nightly 600 pounds of grass.

And so it went on. From Mbeya to Mpanda we flew along the wonderland of Lake Rukwa, dodging the columns of pelicans riding the thermals bubbling up from the floor of the valley.

From Tabora our track to Nairobi lay across the Serengeti. I spent my first local leave there. You picked up a ranger at the Ngorongoro Crater and he guided you to Seronera for there was no real road in those days. You crossed Olduvai Gorge much further down than you do now, went round by the shifting sands and then headed in the general direction of the high ground on the western edge of the plains. I think the chap I had must have gone astray somewhere because I can distinctly remember that when we came to Lake Magadi we made a sharp right turn to get to the camp, and that's a long way from where the road runs now. There were two *bandas* – thatched huts – at Seronera then, and I was the only one staying there.

The more I flew around and the more I saw of such magical places the more I wanted to be part of them. By the same token, though, I came to realize that this wasn't so easy. Driving or walking around, just looking, is all right for a while, but it soon becomes apparent that something is lacking. To be an observer isn't enough. Your mind is too active to be satisfied so simply.

It is why, or so I believe, in another time, men became professional hunters. There was the same urge to be out there, to see around the next corner, but unless you can inject some purpose into this kind of existence it's an empty one. There's nothing to be gained from it. You don't take part, you don't participate, you don't belong there at all – you're just an onlooker. And then, of course, there is the small matter of earning a living. And what better way to do it than by putting a bullet into an elephant carrying the big ivory that was common in those days?

Don't misunderstand me. I'm not against hunting as such. In fact I think that hunters – the professionals I mean – have a far greater fundamental understanding and achieve a much higher degree of involvement than most photographers. Nor do I think they inflict more suffering than occurs in the normal course of events. Most of us live nowadays under a system in which we are cushioned from discomfort and pain and death – until our own turn comes. It is all hidden away and so our sense of values tends, at least in this respect, to be a little unreal.

Terrible things happen in nature, causing indescribable suffering, at least as seen through human terms. For instance: I wonder what goes on in the mind of a lion when it kills or a wildebeest as it is dragged down. I don't imagine that anyone will ever find out, but it's a pretty fair bet that the lion's motivation at any rate is hunger. The animal has learned that a zebra or wildebeest represents a means of satisfying the desire for food. Since the target won't stand still and wait to be eaten, you could say in a way that the kill is purely incidental, merely a method of immobilizing supper.

To the lion, the quick, clean kill is convenient but without a doubt, coincidental. Very often, the proceedings are drawn out and horribly messy, terrifying and extremely painful to the victim. In fact, these are circumstances attendant upon the death of most wild creatures. The animal to whom the end comes rapidly and painlessly is fortunate beyond belief, and, having seen something of the way these things come to pass, I am inclined to feel that the form of death meted out by an expert hunter is usually better than would be visited upon the unfortunate victim in nature. This was an opinion I would reinforce time and time again during the filming of *Hunters*.

How I became a Wildlife Photographer

And now, after the hunter, comes the photographer. It is only comparatively recently that camera equipment has become effective enough to be used in the field, and it is even more recent – virtually since the advent of television – that it has been possible to earn a living by using it in this way. So will the cameraman, coming late into the field, be able in future years to hold his head any higher than the hunter or sportsman?

Sooner or later every photographer has to decide how far he is prepared to go towards 'setting up' a subject. Some people would argue that it isn't permissible at all, that everything should be filmed under entirely natural conditions and that anything else is cheating. They forget one thing though: that wildlife photographers have to earn a living like everyone else. They have children to feed and clothes to buy and just because they live in the bush and their office is a tent this doesn't mean that all those things don't have to paid for.

Anyone can sit around for 3 years waiting for something to happen. At the end of that time he may have a fantastic film, but the chances are that his expenses will have been so high that he won't make a profit out of it. And unless you have a lot more cash than I do, if you don't make a profit you don't eat.

People often say to me 'You must have a tremendous amount of patience' – or words to that effect. It is not entirely true. Of course I am patient. But only up to a point. I seldom get bored, for instance, sitting in a hide waiting for something to happen. But if I find myself sitting for longer than I think is reasonable under the circumstances, I soon start wondering if I shouldn't be doing it some other way. Patience is very far from being an entirely unrelieved virtue. In fact there are times when it may amount to little more than stupidity. Adaptability is one of the fundamentals of this business and, as a wildlife photographer, the quicker you realize it the better.

It follows, therefore, that any picture you many have of the wildlife scene that involves a horizon dotted with photographers 'being patient', just doesn't bear much resemblance to reality. It is, after all, denying your inheritance deliberately to do things the hard way. Virtually all the animals you are trying to film come better equipped to survive in their own environment than a human being. Either they are heavier or stronger or faster or more agile, or their senses are better developed than your own. Only in one respect do we have an advantage. We are more intelligent. And if you aren't prepared to make use of that fact, you are unlikely to last very long in the business of wildlife filming.

You can't just sit there patiently. You have to cut corners. You must move things along. But how far should you go?

I once had the job of shooting a story about vultures. Actually it wasn't quite as straightforward as that. The story concerned a scientist who'd come out to Africa to work on vultures, and since vultures are such common birds, and are well known to be so, it seemed to me that it was essential to the story to explain why he was going to such lengths to study them.

The point was that although vultures are common all right, very little is actually known about them and while this is something you can say very simply on paper, what I had to find was a way of saying it on film. Fortunately for me it happened that some time previously Hugo Van Lawick and his wife Jane had discovered that Egyptian vultures used stones to crack open ostrich eggs.

Getting it on film was a different matter altogether. It isn't difficult to find the Egyptian vultures and ostriches are easy enough to come by as well. After that the process slows down quite drastically. First you have to find a clutch of eggs that has been deserted, and finally you sit there, fingers crossed, hoping that a vulture will find the eggs before something else gets them.

Well, if you carry on your business that way, the luck you are leaning on is far too slippery, at least, for me. If you really want to get that film you've no option but to step in and help matters along a bit.

In this particular instance I selected an area in which I knew

I'd find both Egyptian vultures and ostriches. Then I went round the Nairobi curio shops and bought up a supply of ostrich eggs.

I set out bait to attract the vultures, moving it to within range of my hide as soon as I'd got them coming in regularly. Then I substituted eggs for meat, which discouraged the species of vulture I didn't need and left me with the Egyptians happily hurling rocks. Initially I made one or two mistakes, but the whole thing was thought up and finished within 10 days and I honestly don't think that a vulture cracking one of 'my' eggs behaved differently in any significant detail than if an ostrich had left them there. No matter what anyone says I can't see anything wrong in that.

In general terms I think you have to ask yourself 'Am I being honest? Is what I'm showing as close to the truth as makes no difference if, under the circumstances, it's neither possible nor desirable to show an actual occurrence?'

It is the answer to the question that is not so easy to arrive at, because I think it is true to say that there is often a very fine dividing line between honesty and dishonesty, between, if you like, fair play and foul. Whether you cross it or not, consciously or otherwise, depends of course on where you yourself decide it should be drawn.

There are more specific limits than this as far as I am concerned. Any 'setting up' that requires cruelty doesn't fall within them. I wouldn't, for instance, put a chameleon on one end of a branch and a snake on the other and sit back to film what happened. Nor would I deliberately set a leopard onto a baboon for the same purpose. If I was a producer I wouldn't even use that type of material knowingly, since I feel that to encourage the sort of mentality that will do this kind of thing is almost as reprehensible as setting it up in the first place.

Fortunately, in the Special I was starting out to film 'setting up' was not possible nor would it be necessary. In *Hunters of the Plains*, everything would happen for real.

2
On Safari

There is an old saying in East Africa 'Any fool can be uncomfortable on safari', and I often quote it when people raise their eyebrows at the amount of gear we carry when we set off on one of our journeys.

It is surprising what you can put up with if really necessary. But there's no sense in roughing things if you don't have to. I'm not trying to prove to anyone how tough or spartan I am. I'm simply trying to operate efficiently and to do the best possible job for the people who are paying me. And while it may be possible to operate effectively in conditions of great discomfort for a limited period, it doesn't take long before your performance starts dropping particularly if you can't get a decent night's sleep and the food is monotonous and badly cooked.

When I was an airline pilot, the pilot's association in the company I worked for tried for years to get us decent accommodation on night stops and an adequate food allowance. I could never understand the management's attitude. If I owned an aeroplane that cost millions of dollars I would be insisting that the people I was paying to fly it were properly rested between flights. I certainly wouldn't be battling to keep them two to a room in a second-rate hotel without air-conditioning or a decent restaurant. 'Eat at the Bernice Hotel' our crews used to say of one palatial establishment we graced with our presence. 'Eat at the Bernice Hotel. Ten thousand flies can't be wrong.'

On Safari

Well, now that I'm responsible for my own accommodation, while there are any number of factors that may prevent us from being as comfortable as we'd like, and while the dreaded ogre of costs is always lurking somewhere, at least we try to take the bumps out of safari life.

My wife Jenny usually accompanies me on safari, together with our 5 year old daughter Rebecca. And depending on what the work entails I also take a driver and a cook. The driver and the cook each have their own tents. We have one tent to sleep in and one to eat and work in. In addition we have a store tent.

Our two main tents are what is known locally as 'Ngong' tents, that is to say they are made with a built-in ground sheet and a fly-sheet that shades the tent itself and extends to form a 9 foot verandah. The outer ends of the verandahs each have zips sewn into them. We pitch the two facing each other and then zip the two verandahs together. The problem with this is that you have got to be sure you have set them the right distance apart otherwise you get a very tiresome gap of 2 or 3 inches in the middle. The longer you have been travelling, the hotter and dustier it has been, the more tiresome those 2 or 3 inches can become.

This is quite a practical set up. You have got 18 feet of covered space between your day tent and where you sleep. You can set up a table under it and work or eat out there or, if it is raining, walk from tent to tent without getting wet.

I wouldn't mind having bigger tents. The larger ones usually have a rather higher side wall which means you have very much more room inside and don't have to stoop. But all that occupies more space, is heavier to cart around and more difficult to erect. So one way and another I think the Ngong tents are a fair solution to the problem of being as comfortable as possible without running into transport difficulties.

It may seem that we adopt a rather grandiose life-style by taking along a cook and a driver, but what I am there for is to go out and film animals, and while I am doing that I can't be making bread, fetching firewood, washing clothes, and going through all the business of preparing food, something that takes a fair bit longer when you're under canvas than in a kitchen with all mod. cons. The sad fact is that you do not get good pictures sitting around in camp. Where I have to be in order to earn a living is out in the field, not doing the housework.

We live and work close to the Equator. This means that the days vary in length very little. It is usually light by seven, dark by seven. So the time at which I get up in the morning depends not so much on sunrise, but on how far I have to travel to reach the scene of operations. Usually though it is between 5 and 5.30, and on most days, Saturdays and Sundays included, I stay out until it gets dark, returning to camp at around 7 or 7.30. Rebecca usually stays up until I return. But shortly after that she goes to bed and I sit with her and tell her 'Goldilocks and the Three Bears' until she falls asleep, which doesn't, usually, take very long. That is our own special part of the day. I know it will be gone soon enough so I try never to miss it.

Then I have a shower, clean the equipment, re-load magazines and try to get my diary written up before supper. Jenny and I eat together. We discuss the events of the day, keeping a careful ear tuned to *News of the African World* on the BBC. Soon after *News about Britain* I'm almost asleep myself. A fair day's work I reckon, even without the cooking.

When we are in town Rebecca goes to kindergarten in the mornings. While we are on safari Jenny teaches her by a correspondence course based in Mombasa. Though the course is excellent and Jenny has got used to teaching Rebecca, I can't pretend that this is an ideal arrangement. One of the things small children need is other small children and I suppose you could say this is something Rebecca doesn't get enough of. However, for better or for worse, I am a wildlife photographer and that means being out in the blue a lot of the time. We had to make up our minds whether it was best for our daughter to see her father once in a blue moon and go to school regularly or, at least at this stage in her life, come away on safari and spend more time with her parents. Only time will tell whether we were right or not, and there will come a day when she has to go to school, but for the time being, that's the way it is.

Accordingly, a fair amount of Jenny's day is devoted to Rebecca, time which, under other circumstances, she would be able to spend on housework. She also has to find time to keep up with what I write during the day. I'm a prolific note-taker. When there's no action for the cameras I often pass the time in hide or Land Rover noting what I've seen and what I can learn from it.

Films are made to a budget. You sign a contract stating that you'll deliver the goods by a certain date and for a certain price and out of that has to come your profit – or loss. Unless you keep a very careful eye on costs, loss is the most likely result. You may be thinking by now 'How strange. Living in a tent, out in the back of beyond, you can't be bothered over much by day to day spending.' But if I adopt this attitude, this is just where I am likely to come unstuck. I doubt if very many people realize just how expensive filming is nowadays. So much wildlife has disappeared in recent times that you are almost always operating in a game park or reserve or controlled area. In these places, you pay filming fees, entry fees, vehicle fees and camping fees. Then, vehicles wear out; tents are damaged and need repairing. At the time of writing, every roll of film I run through my camera costs about £34, without adding anything on for the cost of actually going out and exposing it. At the end of each week you need to be able to say to yourself: 'My receipts for this project to date are such and such. My outgoings are so much. Has my output over the last 7 days been such that I'm ahead of the game or behind it?' If you don't do this, if you aren't mentally in the picture and you just doodle along getting material as and when it happens, then the point at which you could, or should, change your tactics to accord with the prevailing circumstances may well pass without your being aware of it. Let that happen too often and you're in trouble.

So I simply cannot afford to get immersed in the details of cooking, maintaining vehicles and so forth. Of course, I have to be concerned about all these things. If I'm not, no one else will be. But what you really need is a certain amount of time to sit back and think and make up your mind what, under varying circumstances, you should really do next.

I had an excellent training for all this as a commercial airline pilot. Essentially this sort of mental balancing act is what you are doing in an aeroplane. Between the time when you arrive at the airfield and the point when you've got airborne and the after take-off checks have been completed, you are very busy. Up to the top of climb you have to be pretty attentive too. But after that, on the sort of routes I used to fly, there came several hours of cruising in which most of the work of operating the aircraft and its systems was carried out by the navigator and the flight engineer. As the Captain your job is to let the other crew members get on with their part of the proceedings without constantly peering over their shoulders telling them that they should be doing it some other way. What you are supposed to be doing is figuring out what, under the prevailing conditions, it would be best to do if things start going wrong.

This is why I have a driver. Apart from driving, every evening, when we return to camp, it is the driver's job to check the oil, water, batteries, clean the windscreen and make sure we have enough fuel on board for the following day. I check all is well from time to time, but I have plenty of other things to do which I *don't* want to leave to someone else.

To cart this lot around – four adults and a child, tents, tables, chairs, bedding, food, film, camera equipment and all the rest of it – we have a Land Rover, a Range Rover and a trailer. To be honest, I suppose I ought really to have a second trailer. In theory it would help to spread the load a bit. In practice, though, I know what would happen. The extra space would rapidly get filled up with even more impedimenta.

I use the Land Rover to help transport things, but its prime role is as a camera car. It is not the ideal vehicle. There was a time when the Land Rover was literally the only four-wheel drive car anyone ever saw in East Africa. Now, though, at least in Kenya, you see many more Toyota than Land Rovers. The Land Rover is too slow; it is not so easy to work on; it isn't all that comfortable. As the roads have improved in East Africa, people who need cross-country vehicles have tended to drift away towards Toyotas, largely, I think, because you can travel in safety at considerably higher cruising speeds than the Land Rover permits. Instead of responding to the demand for a faster and more comfortable vehicle in this price range the British have allowed the Japanese to make a big dent in their sales.

The Range Rover we use as personal transport and to tow the trailer. It is an excellent vehicle with a wonderful V8 engine which is relatively economical if driven with some discretion at constant r.p.m. over long distances. We cruise ours at 60 m.p.h. and get about 22 m.p.g. out of it, far better than with the Land Rover. But if you venture over that speed, the consumption rises sharply, due, I suspect, to the increase in aerodynamic drag produced by the large frontal area of the bodywork.

I'm sold on the idea of having rather too much engine as opposed to rather too little. A big, slow-revving, V8 stands up much better to long distance cruising than a small, high-revving engine which is constantly operating close to its limits. I was always told when flying aeroplanes that you should adhere very carefully to the manufacturer's recommendations as far as temperatures, pressures and the other laid-down engine limitations were concerned. It's not that the engine won't cope. It's just that when you are confronted with a real emergency and you have to ask the engine to do more than it was designed to do, that's the time when you don't want it to let you down. So I always let our engines come up to their correct working temperatures before putting a load on them and I throw out oil and oil filters long before I have to. I reckon it is cheap at the price.

As far as handling is concerned, in really wet, muddy conditions there just isn't any comparison between the Land Rover and the Range Rover. The latter is way ahead. If I get off the crown of a steeply cambered road in my Land Rover in order, let us say, to avoid oncoming traffic, it is always touch and go whether it will slide sideways into the bank, from which position it is the devil's own job to extricate it. Under similar conditions with the Range Rover you can pick your line and hold on to it, changing from one side to the other at will.

What I would really like to have though, is all that power in the camera car. In other words, what would suit me very well would be a Range Rover engine in a chassis as tough and strong as the Land Rover's. No doubt if it had been a Japanese product we'd have had Range Rover pick-ups, light trucks and all the rest of it by now. But it seems to me that producing things people want to buy is not what British industry is about nowadays.

Tents give us shelter and vehicles provide us with transportation and as such they provide the essential framework within which we regulate our day to day existence in the wild. How we actually live and do a job of work is another matter altogether.

Living in town you can take a lot for granted. You press a switch when you want electricity, turn a tap to get water or gas. We have similar requirements. We have to be able to work after it gets dark. Half-used tins of food go bad even more quickly in the bush, so we need to run a refrigerator. We have to cook and wash and all the rest of it, but in our case we have to consider not just the use of power, but the provision of it as well.

Take lighting for a start. When I first started filming we used kerosene lamps but the illumination they provide isn't brilliant. They're bulky to carry around and so are the tins of kerosene that go with them. This sort of thing is no problem if you have a truck to accompany you, as a professional hunter does when out on safari with his clients. The hunter will go on a series of such safaris during the course of any one season and each one will entail setting up and striking camp several times. He has a lot of use for a truck. Generally speaking our operation is far more static. More often than not when we move into an area we hope to stay there for several weeks without shifting around. So it simply isn't economic to have a large truck standing about doing nothing all this time. As a result we have to operate on a far simpler level. So bulk, or the lack of it, is an important item on our books. Moreover, the fewer trips to fetch more kerosene and the like, the less we have to spend on petrol. So when I decided to ditch the Tilley lamps, I bought a Honda E1000 generator. It gave us a 240v. supply for lighting and I could charge camera batteries off it as well. But it was bulky. It was also noisy and had to be located some way away from camp if you wanted to hear at night as well as see. Moreover, the price of petrol quadrupled in a very short time. So I abandoned the generator and fitted an extra battery to each car, together with a conveniently located terminal so that I could plug an Everready Type 85 lantern into the car system. This enabled us to light each tent with a fluorescent lamp. It seemed common-sense to use the generating capacity of the two cars. They ran around all day and could as easily charge two batteries as one. So now, in the evening we make use of that energy for other purposes. It makes me feel I am getting rather better value out of the fuel we burn up so copiously during the day.

Whatever else happens or mis-happens to our equipment, the 'sharp end' of the operation is always the Land Rover – the camera car. It makes no sense at all to spend time and money manoeuvring yourself into a position from which you can get the footage you want, only to find that something isn't to hand or your equipment is so awkward to handle that the action you've been waiting for is all over and done with before you can get yourself sufficiently organized to film it. Accordingly, over the years, a fair amount of thought has gone into modifying the Land Rover and fitting it out in such a way that it is easy and convenient to work in. This is not to say that there aren't improvements I would like to make even now, but, by and large, the present set up works fairly well.

The vehicle itself is a long wheel base six cylinder Land Rover with a station wagon body. It has one extra tank and jerrican holders on the front bumper. I can carry 34 gallons of petrol. However, installing the second tank meant that getting at the electric fuel pump became a very awkward and time consuming operation. Since this is not the most reliable of components, I had it modified so that, in effect, it provides me with two independent pumps. I have also had it moved from it's original location, to the floor of the car just in front of the driver's seat. So now I have two pumps in case one breaks down, and if this does happen I can get at it easily. I also carry with me two sets of spare points, which are the components most likely to give trouble. And just to be really on the safe side, I take along a length of plastic tube and some rope. So if I am stuck I can tie one of the jerricans onto the roof and fuel feed by gravity direct to the carburettor.

Electrics are not my strong suit, I'm afraid. An electrical fault has to be of a very simple and very obvious nature indeed before I can figure out what's wrong. So I have paid a fair amount of attention to the electrical system.

When I looked at the wiring installed by the makers I recoiled in horror. Even when I bought a book on the sort of electrical problems you could encounter in a 12 volt system, and using this tried to figure out how I'd go about tracing various faults, there was no way I could unravel the secrets of the wire maze. Fortunately a friend of mine offered to rip out the whole lot and wire up the car from scratch, and so everything is now neat and tidy and all the major components are protected by fuses, instead of the two that are all Rover consider is adequate when the car leaves the factory.

The advantage of having a secondary battery was brought home to me a year or so ago while I was filming cheetah. The grass in the area I was working in was very long and it was almost impossible to locate them even though I knew there were plenty of animals in the vicinity. So I got a friend of mine to come down with a light aircraft and spot for me.

Jenny and I slept in the back of the car. Early next morning, the aircraft was to pass over and if I signalled that I hadn't been able to find the cheetah I was trying to follow, it was to fly off and locate it for me. One day we picked up a female with young cubs. I followed her without much trouble until she settled down for the night. Next morning when we woke she was still there. But when she moved off the car wouldn't start. The battery was flat. When the areoplane came over I managed to indicate what the matter was and the pilot flew off back to camp to get a spare. Then he returned, found a place to land and came down. He carried the heavy battery across to us and we started to install it. While we were doing this he walked back to the aeroplane. Passing close to a tree which he had skirted when staggering over with the battery, he was slightly taken aback when a whole family of lions' heads popped up out of the grass.

After we had started the car, he took off and flew round in search of the cheetah, unfortunately without success. But it didn't matter much anyway, for it was obvious that the other battery was rapidly losing its charge as well. We decided not to stop the car again, but to return to camp to try to sort out the problem. In the end we discovered that there was a short in the starter motor and this was draining the battery. So as soon as time allowed, I had a second battery installed in the car. Now, I can start the engine off either battery, charge either battery, and (via a rheostat) run the camera off either as well. As it is not possible to connect both batteries into the system at the same time, at least if I get another problem like that one, I can't drain both inadvertently. So now I should always have power there to get home.

I carry two spare wheels, as we have frequent punctures in country where thorn bushes are plentiful. I have a 10 gallon water tank as well, and this serves both for drinking and to top up the radiator if need be. And I carry a fair number of 'mechanical', as opposed to electrical spares. All this, together with the photographic gear, tends to make for a rather heavy car, so the rear springs on the Land Rover are extra heavy-duty as well.

When filming I always operate with a driver. I sit in the left-hand seat (like the pilot of an aircraft). The normal passenger door has been removed and a cut-down version substituted. It is much stiffer to take the extra weight of the camera and its mount. This door is clamped firmly to the body of the car because I found that the ordinary latch mechanism wouldn't provide a rigid enough platform.

Above my seat is a hatch. This gives access to another camera position on the roof. When I want to put my head out through the roof, I tip my seat backwards on its hinges. The top of the seat has been reinforced with a metal plate and this rests on the floor so that I can now stand up on the metal platform under the seat without damaging it.

To operate the camera I have a small electrical panel just in front of me. Selector switches on this allow either battery to be used for starting or either to be charged. On the right of the panel there is a socket into which I plug the camera.

In place of the rear seat, I have installed an aluminium tray. This is lined with foam rubber and cut out in such a way as to provide safe storage for the Arriflex fitted with a 400 ft Magazine and 85–250 zoom lens, two Nikon still cameras and an assortment of lenses, adaptors, filters, cleaning materials and such like. In this way I have safely stored, but close at hand, virtually all the photographic equipment I need.

Immediately under the tray are spares for the Land Rover – such things as radiator hoses, fan belts and cans of brake fluid. Other spares are located in a tool box on the front bumper and in a compartment behind the rear seat where all the electrical spares are concentrated.

Finally, in the roof, on either side of the car, two wooden boxes are bolted in and padlocked. These contain the

On Safari

emergency kits, holding canned food, a small gas cooker and spare bottles, matches, medical spares, two space blankets and whatever might be needed to tide us over for a few days in the event of a breakdown. We often operate in remote areas where there is little likelihood of other traffic appearing. The fact that these supplies are always kept in the car would at least give us an option of whether to stay with the Land Rover or start walking. Without them, their would be no choice whatsoever.

That then is the layout of my 'office', where most of the work is done, and of our home where we live and eat and sleep. How we actually operate within that framework is what the rest of this book is about.

3
My Approach to Filming

Just before starting *Hunters of the Plains* I was in England to discuss details with *Survival*. Naturally I watched a lot of telly and not only nature programmes. One night, on a book programme, I watched a gentleman by the name of Pierrepoint. Mr Pierrepoint had, for many years held the post of public executioner. He had just written a book about his experiences. In response to questioning he made the remark, if I remember it correctly, that no matter what the crime involved he considered it his duty to arrange matters so that a man could die 'with dignity'. Very commendable – and I don't mean that sarcastically – but difficult, I would have thought. After all, it can't have been easy to disguise the fact that society having judged the person concerned to be so evil he could no longer be allowed to live, what Mr Pierrepoint was there to do was take him out of his cell and break his neck.

Accidental death is unpleasant enough. It's when you know in advance what is going to happen that you really get that nasty feeling in your stomach. Perhaps I'm squeamish, but I never got used to watching violent death in nature and I could only marvel at the enthusiasm with which visitors to the plains anticipated even the possibility that they might witness one or other of the predators in action. It seemed to indicate how utterly removed from the realities of life so many of us become. At one lodge where I stayed to film hunting dogs, the manager

My Approach to Filming

used to muster the guests who wanted to watch the spectacle and in a suitably jovial frame of mind the group would set out.

I had decided that hunting dogs were my first target for the *Hunters* Special. Hunting dog packs range over a very wide area indeed. Only when they have puppies in a burrow to which you can be sure they will return each day, are their movements in any way predictable. So the fact that this particular pack had a litter meant that people from the camp had a rendezvous at which they could assemble in order to watch the proceedings. The twice-daily ritual took on a somewhat macabre aspect.

Those who witnessed what happened seldom returned for a second time. Indeed, some of those involved didn't manage to sit through a full performance even once. When the excitement of the chase had worn off and it began to dawn on them what was happening, they departed to take in some less colourful aspect of the African scene. I can't say I altogether blamed them. But what, I wondered, had they thought they were going to see in the first place?

It is this curious ambivalence about death that makes a film about predators so tempting to tackle in theory, but so difficult to accomplish in practice. I'll never forget the first time I saw the dogs kill way back in my early days as a wildlife photographer. It was in April, and the short grass plains on the eastern edge of the Serengeti were thick with wildebeest. I was out on an aerial recce of the area between Naabi Hill and the Gol Kopjes. We climbed slowly, taking in the extraordinary sight below, when suddenly, not far off, a great circle appeared in the herds, a sure sign that there were predators about. I swung round and headed for the disturbance. There in the centre of the ring you could see the white tails wagging and the pack trotting along in the early stages of the hunt, with wildebeest in their thousands fanning out ahead.

For perhaps 10 minutes we circled above them as they drove through the migration in a great symmetrical swirl, sometimes stopping for a minute or so, occasionally changing direction, but mostly moving forward at the 15 m.p.h trot that we were soon to know so well. And then they were off. The leading dog accelerated, his speed taking him right into the wildebeest running ahead. He plunged into the mass, overtaking the rear ranks with ease, quite obviously intent now, amongst all those thousands, on one single individual.

Behind followed the pack. A Tommy bounced along with that peculiar stiff-legged gait known as 'pronking'. It passed through them unheeded, for already the first dog was worrying at the heels of an adult wildebeest, harrying it, forcing it to kick, slowing it down until the others caught up and the last of them were, once again, back in the eye of the storm.

To see the dogs destroy a large animal can be a pretty distressing experience. To see any animal killed is unpleasant, even by one of the larger predators capable of doing so, as it were, single-handed. But hunting dogs have nothing like that amount of power. They simply do not possess the weapons to tackle anything the size of a wildebeest and deal with it speedily. And so they set about the business of securing supper in their usual fashion. Twice they had the wildebeest down. Twice it got up. Once it even managed to break loose from its attackers and run for a few yards. But still the slow process of what I can only call eating it alive continued. The unfortunate animal stood its ground now, lashing out with it's hind legs, plunging forward against the dogs, watched by an audience of thousands as a ring of fascinated wildebeest drew in close around the struggle. Finally, apparently with one foreleg broken, the wildebeest went down for the last time and, as it collapsed, a hyena rushed in, grabbed it by the back of the neck and hung on. Around the carcass, for by this time I hope that is all it was, the white tails still bobbed and waved. As we climbed away, circling, not speaking, the dogs suddenly turned on the hyena and the last memory I have was of another great surge spreading through the herds as he turned and bolted for the nearest hole.

I didn't realize it at the time but that was the easiest possible

My Approach to Filming

introduction to the subject anyone could have wished for. The air was calm and we circled with scarcely a tremor. On the ground beneath, their shadows lengthening in the evening sun, the small figures gyrated almost in slow motion, on what seemed like the surface of a billiard table. Only odd hints of the savagery below rose to disturb me. All too soon, though, I came to realize the true significance of the dance we had just witnessed and there were times, after I had signed the contract to make *Hunters*, that I lay awake at night wondering how I could have been so half-witted as to walk into such a situation in the first place. I couldn't even claim I didn't realize what the problems were before I began.

Getting good material on the hunters in action isn't easy at the best of times. You may work your legs off and plan and anticipate, get yourself to the right place at the right time, and have everything function satisfactorily, only to look at the footage afterwards and know that to include such horror in a television programme just isn't on. What you must never lose sight of is the fact that people pay to be entertained, not sickened, and something that may be perfectly acceptable when seen in its natural context, may be perfectly unacceptable when brought into your living room in full colour at tea-time on a Sunday afternoon. There is just no way you can go out there and film the first kill you happen on and leave it at that. What you have to do is look for some means of obtaining material that will show enough of what is happening without, at the same time, revealing too much. And the more I thought about it the more it seemed not just difficult but darn near impossible. So what was it that induced me to commit myself to such a risky proposition at the outset?

Well, the fact is that I am in business to make films about wildlife. And to stay in business I have to make films that people want to buy. No one ever made a good film about scenery. It is moving pictures one is after. And where the action, drama and excitement are to be found most frequently in nature is amongst the predators.

Hunters of the Plains

I suppose it says something for *Survival*'s faith in my ability that they committed themselves to such a venture with no more that a general outline of the story laid down. Nevertheless, I was well aware that anyone who puts money into a film expects, not unreasonably, to see something happening as soon as possible. So when it came to working out a plan of campaign my prime consideration was to figure out at the earliest possible moment how to come up with a good film showing one or other of the predators in action. In my case, partly because I'd filmed both of them before, and therefore had at least some idea what the problems were; and partly because they are both diurnal species – daytime hunters – there were two obvious targets: cheetah and hunting dog. So it was, with these two objectives in mind, that we left Nairobi and set out for Tanzania. Jackal, hyena, and lion would come later. Especially lion. I had no illusions about how difficult it was going to be to film *them* in action.

Now Colin Willock and his team at *Survival* may not agree with me, though, I suspect they will. In my opinion, anyone who writes a detailed script for a wildlife documentary in advance of the actual filming must be out of his mind. It is almost certain to be a waste of time. The cameraman simply doesn't have enough control over his subject to be able to fit film to laid-down script. The more usual procedure is to start with an agreed outline of the story you want to tell and the cameraman then goes out to look for an appropriate way of illustrating the points you want to put over. What he comes back with will depend on a number of factors – his ability, his luck, and the rapport you manage to establish with him over the outline. Give him an outline that he clearly doesn't believe in and you are in trouble. Either he will follow your brief, or he will disregard it altogether and, while the result may be good, the story you end up telling certainly won't be the one you originally had in mind.

I was lucky with *Hunters of the Plains*. We were all agreed on the outline plan. It had to be about the principal predators – dog, hyena, even jackal and, of course, cheetah and lion; and leopard if we were very lucky. It had also to deal with their prey and the reactions of the prey to the hunter, the methods used to evade, escape, hide and, above all, sense danger. But we all knew that the actual incidents that illustrated these themes could not be scripted. Some we could confidently predict. Others would be a matter of luck. The rest was up to me.

My own approach to filming the predators was to start at the other end – with the prey. Each of the hunters we had chosen has evolved along different lines. To understand why this was so and how it affected my film objectives it was necessary to take a close look at the target from the 'hunter's' viewpoints. What was it they were each trying to catch? What defences were they trying to breach?

Each of the prey animals operates in what I think of as a sort of soap bubble within which its senses – sight, smell and hearing – are effective. But let us forget the three-dimensional aspect for the time being, and consider only what happens in just one plane.

The animal is represented by a dot. It stands on a flat, empty plain. The circle drawn around it represents the range of its vision. But its vision isn't equally effective throughout the area covered by the circle. It decreases with distance and depends, to some extent, on whether the object involved is moving or not. Sight is a precise sense. If an animal detects a predator by visual means, by the very nature of things it automatically pin-points its position.

Vision is not modified to any noticeable extent by the strength and/or direction or the wind. This is not so in the case of smell or hearing. Where these senses are concerned, the wind is a big factor and, at least with smell, often extends the boundary of the envelope well beyond the range of sight. Now, if we superimpose the three diagrams one on the other, we get some idea of the basic protection provided by the animal's own senses. It is not, of course, quite as simple as that in practice. The animal is seldom, if ever, standing on a flat plain. Not infrequently the ground is cut up by gullies and covered to a greater or lesser extent by trees and bushes. Each of these creates a 'shadow' within which any object is hidden from sight, although its identity may still be revealed by its scent drifting off down-wind. But within one animal's range of vision may be other animals, each wrapped in its own individual bubble. Thus, when a number of animals are present some, if not all, of these shadows are ineffective.

For example, an individual which has detected a predator within its bubble will, if approached closer than a certain distance, take flight. Up to this point, while regarding the intruder as a threat, the animal may not look upon it as such a threat that it feels the need to move off. But it may well have its alarm system triggered. Its emotional state may be aroused to the point where it starts snorting, stamping its feet or twitching its flanks. These outward manifestations of nervousness are seen and interpreted by its neighbours whose attention is thus drawn to a potentially dangerous situation, even though they themselves may have been unaware of what is going on.

Sometimes the predators will use to their own advantage the fact that if they detect a threat close at hand the prey animals are unable to resist a compulsion to run. I have seen a spotted hyena making use of this tendency very effectively when hunting flamingo. Large numbers of lesser flamingo had bred on a small soda lake. This was now occupied by a vastly increased population of birds of which some were adults and the rest were young as yet incapable of flight. Amongst such a large congregation there were bound to be a certain number of birds that were either sick or injured or partially incapacitated in one way or another.

On one shore of the lake was a fresh-water spring to which the flamingo came when they wanted to drink. The hyena would lie patiently not far from the spring, nose to the ground, looking for all the world like a lump of brown mud. The birds advanced steadily. Soon they were wading in the spring and drinking.

My Approach to Filming

Then the hyena would stand up. Panic! A strange animal is at hand. Those that could fly, flew. Those that could run, ran. The lame and the halt, left behind in the rush, were scooped up by the hyena and eaten.

This is a favourite tactic on the part of the predators. They seldom rush about haphazardly for they have to balance the energy they are likely to expend during the chase against the input they will receive in the event of success. If the former exceeds the latter too often, they are in trouble. On the whole, the contest between prey and predator is quite finely balanced. Move and counter move are well known. And the hunters contemplating an attempt on a herd often study their intended victims at considerable length before deciding whether or not to make the required effort. They look for very young animals that are likely to panic when the attack comes and do the wrong thing. They watch for lame animals, a pregnant female, awkward and slow on it's feet, or an animal showing signs of advanced age.

In this context you can get a fair idea of how effective the various predators are by watching to see the degree of caution they need to exercise in order to penetrate the sense 'bubble' confronting them. The dogs don't seem to bother much. They don't attempt to conceal themselves. Most of the time they simply trot across country not seeming to care whether the prey spots them or not, confident in their ability to run down any animal they see as being a worthwhile target. Surprisingly enough, it sometimes works that way with cheetah as well.

A female cheetah I once filmed had had nothing to eat for 9 days except for one very small gazelle which she had shared with her three cubs. It wasn't entirely her fault. She had actually knocked over an adult gazelle, but this had fallen into a stream where she was unable to retrieve it. On the ninth day she walked out onto an area of open plain and there, some way ahead of her, were two Thomson's gazelle males sticking to their territories. Both saw her and gave their alarm signals.

Hunters of the Plains

Under normal circumstances a cheetah stands little chance of catching a healthy adult gazelle that has received advanced warning of the predator's approach. I had seen her when she was hunting, walk past many gazelle like this without bothering to make even a token attempt at a chase. But on this occasion, although she ignored the first male gazelle and strolled casually past him, she suddenly rushed at the second.

It was the longest chase I ever saw. She ran on and on until finally the gazelle appeared in the viewfinder just ahead of her and over he went in a cloud of dust. She got him. When I looked at the film afterwards I saw he had actually fallen over before she reached him, perhaps out of sheer exhaustion, for his horns were worn right down and it was obvious that he was a very old animal. It was a pity to see him go, but a good example of the way the theoretical model is modified in practice.

There was nothing wrong with the gazelle's bubble, its warning system. But once the cheetah had spotted the tell-tale signs of age, its fate was sealed. The hunter had the edge and used the weapons that heaven alone knows how many thousands of years of evolution had bestowed on her for just that purpose.

And that's the way it goes. The predators maintain the pressure on the herds that ensures that only those capable of surviving do survive. What the cameraman is there to do is look for material that will show just that. To get what I wanted I felt I had to study the prey at least as closely as the predators. That way I had a chance of predicting the forthcoming action and of being in the right place to film it.

4
The Search for the Right Pack

At the beginning of 1977 there were six known packs of hunting dogs using the plains that formed the eastern part of the Serengeti National Park and the adjoining section of the Ngorongoro Conservation Area. In addition, a small group of three, previously unrecorded adults had been spotted not far from Ndutu. Ndutu is the site of a lodge beside the small soda lake Lgarya. So the potential target was a total of perhaps 35 to 40 dogs spread out over an area of some 4,200 square kilometres.

But we were not looking for just *any* pack. I couldn't afford to spend 90 per cent of my time driving around the plains in the hope that I would occasionally catch sight of a pack from which, with luck, I might extract a few feet of film. What I needed was a static situation, a location to which I could drive every day and be reasonably certain I would find dogs doing something that I could film. In practice, what that meant was a pack with puppies at a den. The point was, of course, how to find one.

A dog pack with small puppies is in much the same position as a bird with young in the nest. If it is to provide its offspring with the protection they need and the food they require it cannot fly too far away. So there is no point in nesting at a time of the year when an adequate food supply doesn't exist within the chosen area. A similar consideration applies to hunting dogs. And the time most favourable to the plains packs in this respect seemed to be during the rains when the grassland is occupied by vast numbers of antelope, especially wildebeest and gazelle, on which they can prey with relative ease.

A pack of dogs on the move amongst a large gathering of wildebeest creates an effect somewhat akin to the Rev. Ian Paisley arriving unannounced at Canterbury Cathedral during a Bishop's Convocation. Suddenly everyone discovers they have urgent business elsewhere. This is all very well as long as you are standing on the steps of the cathedral at the moment of truth. But you wouldn't have to be more than a couple of streets away to be in complete ignorance of what was going on only a very short distance from you. Much the same applies to an observer on the ground out on the plains. Your visibility is very restricted indeed. So to overcome this difficulty I planned to use an aircraft. What I hoped to do was fly over the herds morning and evening, that is to say at those times when the dogs were most likely to be out and about, and to locate them by watching for the disturbance they caused when they started hunting. The idea was to base myself close to Ndutu Safari Lodge. From December to May when the wildebeest are out on the plains, Ndutu is right in the midst of the action. Every day, people from the lodge would be driving out to look at the animals. So, if hunting dogs were sighted, I should inevitably hear about them.

Anyone with experience of working in Africa will, by now, have a sceptical smile on his face. Well, all I can say in reply is that there was no harm in trying. It ought to have worked. The only trouble was that, 2 days after we arrived at Ndutu, a dispute arose between Tanzania and Kenya. The border between the two countries was closed. Any Kenya-registered aircraft on the ground in Tanzania were confiscated. It was a period of great uncertainty, a very worrying time. Moreover, not only did it become impossible to use an aeroplane, but the

The experts say that the most effective hunting unit is two adult females operating together.

'I had to find the ideal pride to concentrate on. At first, the Tokitok Ten seemed to fill the bill.'

Many of the kills in the Ngorongoro Crater are made by hyena. The lions often stole from them.

Hyena live in organised clans with well-defined territories. They attack any intruder fiercely.

flow of visitors to Ndutu ceased. All the extra pairs of eyes and ears that I had been counting on to help me vanished over night. Moreover I was by no means certain that I would be allowed to stay and film. Quite apart from all this there was the whole question of communications. Jenny was still in Nairobi. How would I get supplies if friends could no longer fly in from Kenya?

So there I was, upside down, with both engines shot away and a silly expression on my face. In retrospect, I must admit to having experienced a slight twinge of panic at this point. But fortunately it wasn't long before my sense of proportion began to reassert itself. When I flew aeroplanes to earn my living, one of the things I learned was that there is nothing so much of a menace as a pilot who, when things begin to go wrong, starts pushing buttons. Unless you are absolutely sure what the problem is, you stand at least a 50 per cent chance of pressing the wrong buttons. 'When in doubt, do nowt', is not a bad maxim to follow at such times. That doesn't mean you can afford to stay with your brain in neutral for ever, but a brief period of masterly inactivity seldom does anyone any harm. My time as a co-pilot – 'a mouse learning to be a rat', as they say – had convinced me that the captains I flew with who had the greatest reputations for coolness under pressure were those who had the least idea what to do at the time, but had developed the most effective system for concealing this from the rest of the crew.

Doing nothing is not easy, though, and in this respect I was fortunate that I had the *Eternal Triangle* half-hour to be going on with, otherwise I might have been tempted in to some course of action I'd later have regretted. I had enough film stock for the moment. At least, working on scenes other than dogs for the 'Triangle' gave me a breathing space. It was during this period that an event ocurred which in the end was to save the day.

The road to Ngorongoro crosses Olduvai Gorge, some 60 miles from Seronera. This is an area that has excited scientific interest since before the First World War, although serious

Hunters of the Plains

anthropological work on a sustained basis only began there as recently as 1952.

The significance of the Olduvai as an anthropological workshop is more immediately apparent from the air than it is from the ground. From above, the uneven surface of the stony plain recedes to become a smooth, greyish-green tableland that looks for all the world like a filling poured into the space between the Ngorongoro Massif and the mountains of the Ol Doinyo Gol. Through this, with quite extraordinary abruptness, the canyon slashes like a deep wound gouged out of the high plateau; a gigantic cross-section through some 2 million years of history.

A long time ago – a very long time, even by geological standards – this ground was covered by an ocean. Into it rivers flowed, and the deposits they laid down on the sea-bed, acted upon by pressure, and undergoing chemical changes, produced rocks. Eventually, as the waters receded, these appeared above the surface. At that point, other forces came into play. Atmospheric erosion commenced. Gradually the topmost layers were ground away until only the most ancient crystalline rocks that had formed deep down beneath the earth's crust remained as mountain ranges still standing above the level of the surrounding plains. And the Ol Doinyo Gol, or Gol Mountains to give them the name by which they are more usually known, are an example of such a range.

And then, not far east of the Gols, some 25 million years ago, a fracture appeared in the earth's surface. This resulted in the ground there subsiding some 3,000 feet below it's original level, and the immense pressures caused by this faulting gave rise to considerable volcanic activity. Great quantities of lava poured out of the ground east of the fault line. Slowly the difference between the two levels was reduced and in the end, the valley was completely filled in. But in the course of this levelling process, the cracks through which the lava had flooded began to seal, and the outlets for the molten material seething below became restricted to a series of holes or vents. These, or what is

The Search for the Right Pack

left of them, you can see to this day in the Crater Highlands around Ngorongoro. The origin of the present day Olduvai is very closely associated with the upheavals that resulted in the formation of these highlands.

For many years a lake existed at the foot of the Ngorongoro range. Its level fluctuated considerably. During periods of heavy rainfall it rose, while at others it became little more than a swamp as a rain of ash and other volcanic debris descended on it from some upsurge of activity in the highlands towering immediately to the east. Finally, about 150,000 years ago, a further period of faulting took place. One result of this was the formation of the depression at Ol Balbal which still exists today. Whatever water lay in the lake at that time drained away into the Ol Balbal and that was the end of Olduvai as a lake. From then on, any water draining into it from the higher ground to the west passed on through to collect in the lower depression instead. In doing so it cut deep into the soft deposits of the old lake bed and began to form a valley.

But the valley didn't last long for at about that time the volcano, Kerimasi, began to make its presence felt. Indescribable quantities of ash began billowing from its cone. They cover the Sale Plains to this day and they put paid to the beginnings of the new valley as well. But eventually Kerimasi ceased erupting. Once again the process of erosion commenced and the formation of a gorge began which would one day reveal the traces left behind by early or near man, as he lived and died under the shadow of the Crater Highlands rumbling and muttering so close at hand.

Looking down from the Highlands at the Ol Balbal, the Olduvai, the Sale Plains and the ancient mass of the Gols, I defy anyone to remain unmoved at this glimpse into our own remote past. No one can do more than guess at the changes that have taken place out there over the years. But to stand in the gorges of the Gols where the griffon vultures nest and listen to the rustle of their wings echoing against those rocks that rose from the sea so long ago; to lie on the hills that flank the Angata Kiti – the high, remote pass through the Gols – and watch the long files of wildebeest plodding on down towards the Sale Plains, heads held low against the blowing sand that once burst from the cone of Kerimasi far off to the east, is to be, for a short while, part of a landscape which has something of Creation itself wrapped round it.

At the entrance to the Angata Kiti there stands a rock the Maasai call Nasera. To the best of anyone's knowledge its overhang has been used by hunter-gatherers for at least 10,000 years. On 5 March, Aajte ('Inky' for short) Geertsema, a Dutch girl who was working at Ndutu studying Serval cats, took her parents and some friends from Arusha across to the Gols for the day. Quite why she went there at just that time I do not know. But anyway, that afternoon they came across 1 female and 3 male hunting dogs. She recognized them as belonging to the Genghis Pack, so called by Jane and Hugo Van Lawick when studying them a few years previously. They were Marcus, Homer and Jinja, accompanying their breeding female Kali. Inky followed them until they settled into the den where, shortly afterwards, Kali was to give birth to her litter of thirteen pups. Jinja, Inky reported, wore a radio telemetry collar placed there some time ago by the Serengeti Research Institute and long since non-operational. I thought that the presence of this might prove to be a nuisance when filming them – it would hardly look wild or natural – but decided I would face that when it happened.

It was, to say the least of it, a monumental piece of luck. A day earlier or later, even an hour's difference in timing, and in all probability the pack would have denned and had their puppies out there in the wilderness and no one would have had the faintest idea they were there.

Two days later, following the instruction I'd been given on how to find them, I went across to see for myself. As we came over the ridge and drove down the slope on which the den was supposedly located, Marcus, the dominant male, got up from where he'd been lying and came over to inspect us. Homer rose looked at us briefly, and lay down again. Jinja was there too. He had a collar on, just as I had been told, and there was no mistaking it. But the transmitter with which it had originally been fitted had gone. It certainly wasn't as conspicuous as it must have been at one stage and it seemed that I could film without showing it. Of Kali, there was no sign. But this in itself was a hopeful omen. If she really was as far advanced in pregnancy as Inky had suggested it was more than likely that she would be below ground. The fact that we couldn't see her tended to confirm that the dogs had indeed settled into a den.

The journey back to Ndutu that evening was a cheerful one. Locating the Genghis Pack in such a way could hardly be called anything but luck. And finding them in an area so favourable to photography was a lot more than that, it was unbelievable. After all the worries and uncertainties brought about by the border closure it seemed as if our fortunes might have begun to change at last. If so, as far as I was concerned, it wasn't a minute too soon.

When you are watching hunting dogs it is an unusual day when something interesting or exciting doesn't happen. And, of course, interesting and exciting happenings are the very stuff of which natural history programmes are made. On their own, though, they are not really enough.

Not long after starting work on *Hunters* I went to see a film about dogs that someone else had made. It was an enjoyable evening, although the film was frankly bad. Not that I enjoy watching bad wildlife films, but from them you learn so much more. In a good programme you may see one or two moves you admire and try to remember for possible future use. But in a bad one you see the mistakes projected with such appalling clarity that you never, ever, forget them.

This particular film was a good illustration of these points and on looking at the individual takes I hoped I would do as well. But no matter how good its constituent parts were, the story itself was totally confusing. But of course, it's easy to criticize. The difficult part is to come up with something better.

When you set about filming a pack of dogs with pups you known certain things are going to happen with absolute certainty. The dogs will hunt; feed the pups; the pups will play, and so on. You will see this sort of thing repeated time after time. The only real problem here is not to over-shoot. It is tempting to go on covering the action over and over again in the hope that by doing so you will get something just a little different or a little better, but there is no point in doing so. Moreover, it is extremely costly and the finer points of behaviour that your over-shooting may have captured do not compensate for this and may not even find their way into the finished film!

Then come the less-predictable events. If the dogs move to a new den, the female may carry some of her offspring to their new home. This can provide you with a very good sequence indeed . . . if you can get it. But it is not something you can be sure will happen. At best, all you can do is to be aware of the possibility and hope you can capture the moment if and when it comes. What you watching for all the time are the totally unpredictable things . . . a hunt, say, in which the victim turns on the predators and for once succeeds in driving them off. But you are unwise if you rely on such happenings. The deciding factor here is undoubtedly luck and luck is a very slippery commodity indeed.

Your job, as a professional, is to come back with material from which a better than just superficial programme can be made. If you get something out of the ordinary, all well and good. If you don't, you still have to bring in a programme. So what you are constantly looking out for is some way to transform the ordinary material you *know* you can get, into something rather better than has been done before.

To my way of thinking the really interesting thing about

The Search for the Right Pack

hunting dogs is their ability to co-operate. Any fool can compete, but it takes a certain amount of intelligence to work with another individual, not against him. To achieve this end an animal has to be capable of communicating; has to have, if you like, a vocabulary. The trouble is that many of the attitudes and gestures the dogs use to pass information back and forth between themselves are of an extremely fleeting nature. More often than not it is all over and done with very quickly and you can't keep running the film back and forth in case the audience missed whatever it is you are trying to get over to them. You have to slow the action down or 'freeze' it, an optical process at the laboratory stage, so that people catch on the first time round. Unless you do this you cannot hope to bring to the screen anything more than just another bunch of dogs trotting back and forth, doing all the things that wild dogs are known to do.

Throughout the time I filmed them, the dominant male of the Genghis Pack was Marcus. I know some people would argue that there is no such thing as a good-looking hunting dog, that they all look mangy and half-starved, that their eyes are so flat and lifeless they can never look anything but killers. I don't agree. I will not deny that Marcus had a rather menacing appearance and to look into his eyes for any length of time was a somewhat disconcerting experience. Nevertheless there was a vitality about him that I found impressive. He was almost completely black. Even from a distance, his springy gait and alert attitude proclaimed him for what he was, a young, confident male not quite old enough to be in his prime, but a formidable animal for all that.

The previous history of the Genghis Pack had been well documented by Hugo and Jane Van Lawick* and others.

Marcus was born in to the Genghis pack in mid-1974, one of a litter produced by a female called Havoc. In fact, this was to be Havoc's last litter, for in December that same year she died as

* See their book *Innocent Killers* (Collins)

the result of an injury to her jaw, probably received while out hunting. It was this accident that left the Genghis Pack without a female and opened the way for the arrival of Kali and her sisters. In the months ahead, Kali would mate with Marcus. When I filmed them she was the dominant female, but this was not a situation that came about immediately.

Kali came from the Semetu Pack. Amongst hunting dogs the mechanics involved when the members of an established group split up are not as well understood as is the case, for example, with lion. Lion organize themselves in such a way that their family groups, or prides, are almost always based on a hard core of females. When they are about 2 years old, the young males leave the group to become nomadic. Occasionally they will attach themselves to a pride, an arrangement that may last for a few weeks, for some months, or even in extreme cases for a year or so, but their association with the females is almost always no more than temporary. After a while, they move on again.

In dog society, though, the system is by no means so clearly defined. Both males and females migrate. Sometimes a male and female may even go off together. But precisely what happens seems to depend more on the circumstances prevailing at the time than on any set pattern of behaviour, as with lion.

In theory, at any rate, each pack has only one breeding female. She alone mates and produces puppies. Eventually, the females from the litters to which she gives birth leave the group, although quite what triggers off these moves is not known for sure. What does seem certain, though, is that hunting dogs are able to tell when there is a group of males in the area currently unaccompanied by a female. So it seems possible that in this case the paths of the Genghis and Semetu Packs crossed at some point and the subordinate Semetu females, well able to 'read' the scent marks left behind by the Genghis males, recognized the opportunity awaiting them as a result of Havoc's death and decided the time had come to break away.

When females migrate they have usually decided amongst

The Search for the Right Pack

themselves which is 'top dog' or rather top bitch. When they reach the males, only a very short time elapses – sometimes no more than a few minutes – before it becomes clear which pair will assert reproductive dominance. But in this instance, when the Semetu sisters and the Genghis males came face to face, the pair that formed was not Kali and Marcus, but Kali and Homer.

It may have been coincidence, of course, but, not long after Kali joined them, the Genghis pack began to appear less frequently in their old haunts. It was almost as if she was reluctant to leave the ground with which she must have become familiar in her wanderings with her former companions, the Semetu pack. Previously, the Genghis pack had been fairly regular visitors to the Ndutu/Naabi Hill area. But in June 1975, having successfully established herself in the new group, Kali settled into a den a good 40 miles away to the north-east. Presumably she had pups there, although how many is not known, and in any case none of them survived the denning period. After this, though, the make-up of the pack changed rapidly.

By September both Kali's sisters had disappeared and by December, not only had Marcus' siblings vanished as well, but Swift, another of the Genghis males, was also dead. At this point too, Marcus managed to supplant Homer as the breeding male. Quite what caused this upheaval . . . for upheaval it must certainly have been . . . isn't known. One possibility could have been disease, for Marcus is the youngest male ever known to have taken over the dominant role in this way and it may be that he managed this feat because Homer was sick and as a result was unable to stave off his challenge.

Although you'd never know it to look at them, Homer and Jinja are brothers. They were born on or about 1 August 1969, to Juno, who was herself a sister of the dominant female Havoc. So when we caught up with them, thanks to Inky, they were by no means young dogs. But while there was no mistaking the fact that Homer was older than Marcus you certainly wouldn't have thought he was the same age as Jinja. To me, Jinja was the very picture of a subordinate male. He seemed to have a totally resigned air about him, and in both his attitude and his actions he appeared the complete 'underdog', the low man on the totem pole. On the other hand it was noticeable that Homer never lost an opportunity to stand beside Kali, his erstwhile mate. You got the distinct impression that Homer had by no means given up hope of mating again and, as a consequence, was exerting considerable pressure on Marcus. Jinja, by contrast, wasn't exerting pressure on anyone. Some of these relationships I hoped to be able to portray on film.

For instance, the result of all this could be seen in the rather bad-tempered exchanges that not infrequently passed between the two rivals. Mind you, the bad temper, or at least the outward manifestations of it, were all on Marcus' side as far as I could see. Homer's part in the proceedings was simply to act out his subordinate role. I knew that there was not the slightest chance of being able to include the finer aspects of the struggle in a televison programme. But I thought I might get enough 'large' actions out of it that could be used in the context of a 'This is Marcus . . . this is Homer . . . and of the two Marcus is dominant' kind of sequence!

I think you have to try these things, even if they make you unpopular back at base because you are using too much film and no one can understand what it is all about. But a wildlife cameraman is not just a mechanical recorder of events. If he does his job properly, he is also an interpreter. So he needs to back up this kind of shooting with shot-lists, 'dope sheets' and as much written background as he can give. Later when the picture was being cut I knew that I would get together with the *Survival* team in London. Then all the finer points of the Special could be hammered out between us.

The main thing was that we had found our ideal pack, even if it was a small one, and were at last off the ground.

5
Mishaps and Maasai

Wildlife filming is a business and the more you can organize yourself so that fewer problems arise, the more successful you will be. There are enough unknown factors built into the game about which you can't do anything very much, without creating any unnecessary difficulties.

There are two things, above all, that you need to keep an eye on around camp – fuel and food. In 17 April I was nearly out of both. I shouldn't have let myself get so low of course, but filming with the dogs was going well and when that happens the last thing you want to do is spoil your luck. So when I finally decided I couldn't hold on any longer, I did my best to minimize the departure from our normal routine.

'What we'll do', I said to my driver, David, 'is this. On Sunday we'll get everything together. Fill the Range Rover. Load a 44 gallon drum in the back and tie it down. Tools, mail, anything to go to Ndutu we'll load on Sunday. Then on Monday we'll go out and film the early hunt. Once that's finished I'll come straight back, climb in the car and go. I'm not going to hang around Ndutu. I'll just load up, come straight back and we'll go out again and film in the evening.'

At first, all went well. The dogs performed on schedule and by 7.45 I was well on my way to Ndutu. Nothing of note happened crossing the plains. It took me an hour to reach the Park boundary, which was about average. Then I turned left

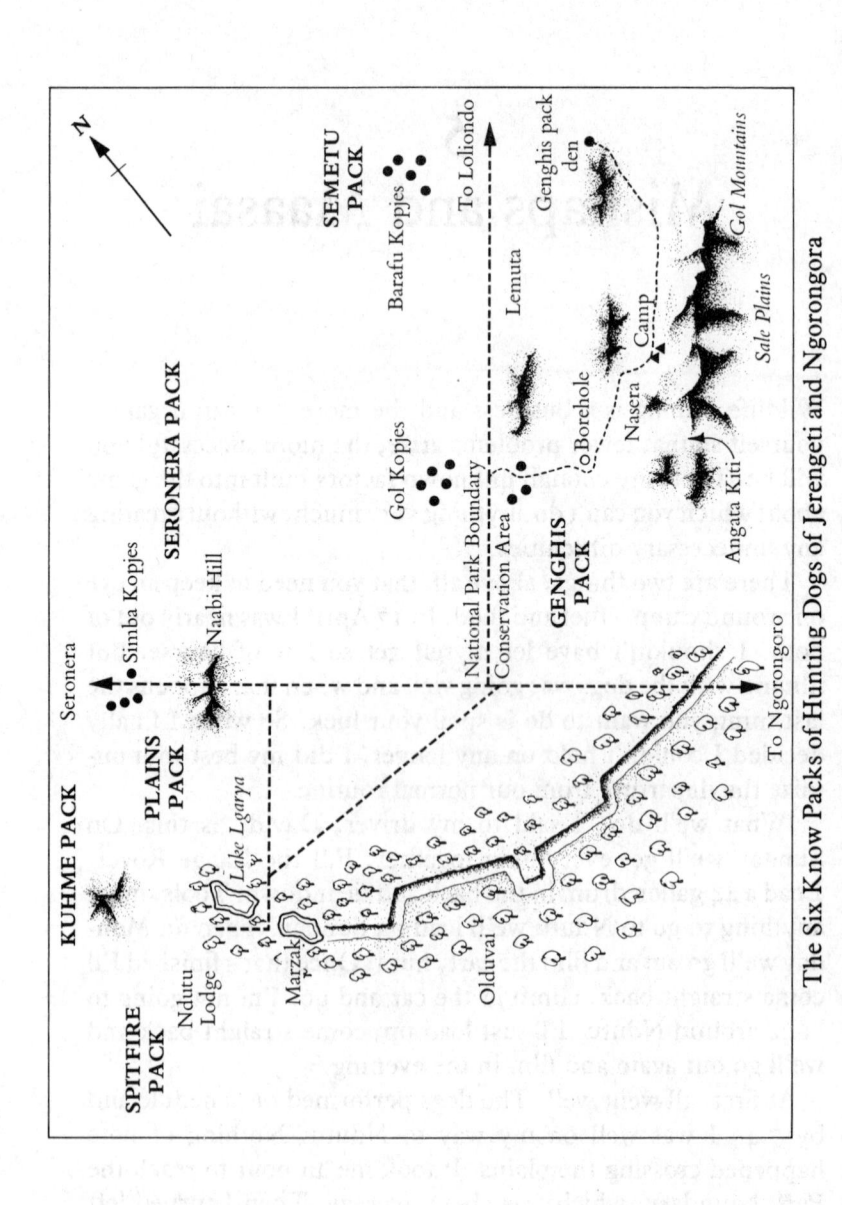

Hunters of the Plains

The Six Know Packs of Hunting Dogs of Jerengeti and Ngorongora

and followed the track as far as the main Ngorongoro-Serona road. There were a few puddles along the way but nothing more. By the time I reached the woodland along the edge of the Olduvai, though, it was downright slippery and I began to remember the big black thunderclouds that had hidden the sun during the evening hunts over the past few days. But nothing prepared me for the Olduvai Gorge itself.

There is a causeway that runs through the bottom of the gorge between Lake Lgarya on your right and Lake Marzak on the left. Actually, you'd have to be told it was a causeway to recognize it as such because it only stands a couple of feet above the level of the ground, a fact that tells you all you need to know about the amount of water that normally lies in the gorge even after really heavy rain. Now there was no sign of any causeway. I stopped at the waters' edge and got out. It was like a sea. Clearly there was no point in even thinking about driving across. But was it worth trying to go round Marzak? My memories of that end of the valley were of swampy ground, so I climbed back into the car and set off round Lgarya instead.

There are two arms of the main lake to cross if you want to skirt Lgarya and reach Ndutu by this alternative route. The first wasn't a problem. The water was a little higher than usual, but the ground below was firm. Over I went. Then came the second crossing. When you get that far you are almost within sight of the lodge. In fact you can often hear people talking there. But the water was so high there was no point in going on. So I reversed a short distance and then turned off the track at a point where I'd crossed a few weeks back while out looking for cheetah. From the look of the ground, which was muddy with vehicle tracks, plenty of other people had had the same idea. Good. I pressed on. The water petered out and I turned left and crossed the valley on dry ground. Once again, the vehicle tracks turned left. I turned with them. Ahead of me now I could see the water gleaming in the grass. On my right, the side of the valley rose up steeply but not so steeply that I couldn't get up.

Hunters of the Plains

Perhaps that was the best way. What the hell. Everyone else had gone along the edge, why shouldn't I? Why waste time. I was an hour late already. The Range Rover is such a good vehicle in wet conditions that there is only one way you can really get stuck and that is to sink in so far that the chassis is in contact with the ground. And within 30 seconds of pressing on that is exactly what had happened.

A passing Thomson's gazelle spooked at the stream of bad language. Still, at least I had two jacks, blocks of wood to stand them on, a spade and so forth, so I jumped out and got to work. Not far off I could hear people at the camp talking and revving up motors and there was a considerable temptation to go and ask for a tow. But no. It is bad enough to get stuck by acting like a half-wit. One doesn't want to advertise the fact. So I got to work jacking and digging and fetching and carrying. It took me a whole sweat-stained hour to get clear. But at least I was mobile again, no one had seen me, and I was within 5 minutes of camp. I broke all records over the last mile or so and roared into the car park determined to get a quick turn round. If I could be on my way again within the hour I could still get back to camp on schedule.

The manager, Inayat Anjari, waved from the window of his office and came out to greet me. We exchanged pleasantries and I explained my position. 'I've got a list of stuff I hope you'll be able to let me have: flour, butter, rice . . .' I went down the list and he looked over my shoulder as I read. 'We've got everything', he said 'except tinned meat. We're right out of meat.' I groaned. The prospect of living for the next couple of weeks on cans of curried beans, which I knew were the only alternative, was hardly enthralling. Still, we would survive. I put a ring round item 19 on my list 'meat', and drew a line through it. I was still standing there recovering from this blow to my morale when the manager fired his second broadside.

'I hope you don't need any petrol?' he said.

I stared at him for all of 15 seconds, not knowing quite what to say. 'Yes, yes that's one thing I do want,' I replied. 'You don't mean to tell me you haven't got any? What about all those 44 gallon drums you had when I was here last?'

'While I was away on leave,' he said, 'our storage tank leaked. And when I got back I was just in time to stop them pouring the last of those drums in to replace it, the stuff that already leaked away.'

I was so taken aback all I could do was stand there like an idiot and repeat what he'd just told me.

'The tank leaked?'

'Yes.'

'And when the level fell they poured those spare drums in to top it up?'

'Yes.'

'I don't believe it. You're pulling my leg.'

'Come and have a drink,' he suggested. 'You aren't in any hurry are you?'

'Well, there was a time about 5 minutes ago when I thought I was,' I answered. 'But now you might well be right.'

Before long though, my feeling of dismay began to recede. After all, Ndutu wasn't the only place that had a pump. I could get petrol either at Seronera or Ngorongoro. It would involve a delay of course, but that couldn't be helped.

'Look, I'll tell you what,' I said, in a somewhat happier frame of mind. 'If you can get my order ready this afternoon, I'll go to Seronera early tomorrow and then drive to camp from there. I'll lose two hunts but still . . .'

The manager shook his head. 'You can't get fuel at Seronera either. Now they aren't getting any money from tourists, they don't have the cash to pay for more and they've run out.'

By this time I was becoming immune to shocks. 'OK. then, I'll go to Ngorongoro. In fact, if you can get that order ready now I'll go to Ngorongoro tonight, sleep in the car, and be on my way back to camp first thing tomorrow.'

The manager looked at me as if I was not far short of mad, but he was too polite actually to say so and went off without further ado to get my things. When these came I started loading them into the car. While I was about this, Rashid, one of the Ndutu drivers, came up.

'Salaama.'

'Salaama.'

'Is it wet at your camp?'

'No,' I replied, 'It's dry. We could do with some rain though. Nearly all the wildebeest have left.'

Rashid looked sympathetic. 'It's very wet here,' he said.

'Yes,' I agreed. 'Give me a hand with this box will you?'

He helped me lift it into the back of the car. 'Are you going back to camp now?' he asked. 'It's getting late.'

'Tomorrow,' I said. 'Right now I'm going to Ngorongoro to get petrol.'

Rashid shook his head. 'The road is very bad. I went that way this morning trying to get to Endulen and there were five big lorries stuck in the mud. There's no way to get past.'

It was at this point that I began to feel perhaps I did need a drink after all. I thanked Rashid for his information and headed for the bar. I knew it wasn't going to do my morale much good, for Ndutu in the wet weather can be a pretty gloomy place if there are no visitors around. But still, there was nowhere else to go.

Inayat was at the counter immersed in his accounts. 'Where is everyone?' I asked. Even when there are no visitors at Ndutu there are usually one or two people to be seen, since a number of researchers from SRI are also based there. Now, though, apart from Inayat and myself, there wasn't a soul in sight.

'Jerry and Suzie are out somewhere. I don't know where. Patti was here just now. Hugo came back yesterday and he is stuck in the mud with his friends. I've sent the tractor to pull him out, and Inky and Pradip are down at Marzak trying to find a new road.'

'Perhaps I should get on with accounts as well,' I thought. To hell with bloody accounts. I got out my book: *Destination Disaster*. It seemed like a good choice at that time, and I settled down to read.

After about an hour I heard footsteps. It was Inky back from her trailblazing expedition. She sat down and we exchanged news.

'You know they have no petrol here?'

'Yes I found that out.'

'What are you going to do?'

'Well, I intended to go to Ngorongoro, but Rashid tells me the road is blocked. Since I've only got just enough fuel to get there I suppose the sensible thing to do is sit here for a couple of days until the road dries out a bit and I can be sure I'll get through.'

'Won't that upset your filming?'

'Too right,' I answered with some feeling, 'but there's damn-all else I can do.'

Inky looked over her shoulder. Then she leaned forward. 'I have a 44 gallon drum locked in my store,' she said, very quietly. 'If you swear you'll replace it by next week you can have that.'

The following morning, all arrangements for the replacement of Inky's petrol having been agreed, I set out for camp. There was no point in hurrying. The Range Rover with its load of fuel and food was pretty well weighed down and I picked my way around the potholes and past the worst of the mud as safely as I knew how. As long as I got back in time for the afternoon hunt, that was all that mattered.

In fact, the dogs didn't hunt that evening, but I was so relieved at being back and at having an adequate supply of fuel, when I could so easily have been sitting at Ndutu, that it didn't worry me unduly.

Next morning we were out extra early. No kill the previous night meant that the pack would probably be up and doing well ahead of their usual time and I didn't want to miss them. We drove across from camp with our headlights on. Before we reached the ridge overlooking the den, I got David to switch them off. I didn't want to run any risk of scaring the dogs.

We crawled down the hill in the dark and stopped at a point from which I estimated we'd see the den when it got light. For about 10 minutes we sat, shivering. It was damn cold. Then I heard a familiar sound . . . ears flapping . . . almost certainly Kali had emerged from the burrow. I listened hard for the sounds of greeting. Nothing. Then Marcus came up the hill, stared at the car briefly and went on towards the ridge. I turned the car. The sky was a beautiful cold steely blue and as the four dogs went over the top I filmed them in silhouette. It looked good. As soon as they'd gone, we started up and went after them. Now it was light enough to see our own tracks and we hurried to catch up.

Over the top we went and down the other side. Then I noticed a commotion. The dogs were dancing around something just by the side of the track; something which we must have come close to running over in the dark. It was a very large, very full, and rather evil-looking lioness. What she was lying next to was the carcass of a partly-consumed Maasai donkey.

My heart sank. Anyone who knows anything about the Maasai will realize they would never write off a stray donkey without sending people out to look for it. And when they found it had been clobbered by a lion, that would be an excuse for every layabout from here to Timbuctoo to get in on the act. Everyone would want to come and examine the spot where the dirty deed was done. It was impossible to believe that in the process someone wouldn't stumble onto the den.

It was not the happiest of prospects. But there was nothing I could do about it. The immediate problem was to position myself in such a way that if there was to be a further encounter between the pack and the lioness in light which would permit me to film, at least I would be well placed to cover it. After only a short pause the dogs departed. I wasn't worried about the lioness. She was so full of meat she wasn't going anywhere, so I turned and went after the dogs. As one they made a bee-line back to the den where they all curled up in a tight group and apparently went to sleep. We drove up onto the ridge until we were 100 feet or so above the den. From that position I could keep watch on both parties without disturbing either. A bitterly cold wind blew in through the open side of the Land Rover. Despite my anorak and two thick sweaters I still felt frozen.

Time passed. I gazed down from on high. The lioness remained by the donkey. The dogs made no move away from the den. But although it was irritating to have missed the morning hunt, I must say the view was magnificent. Wrapped around the end of the ridge a vast amphitheatre lay beneath us. While I'd been away at Ndutu the wildebeest had returned in force and now a truly massive movement was under way from the general direction of the Gols towards Lemuta. With the sun still low on the horizon, each animal pushed a long shadow ahead of it. Fold upon fold of undulating grassland rolled away into the distance, each successive wave of slope sharply outlined against the next as the sun lit up one ridge after another. I set up the camera and began to film. Since the prey species were being so obliging as to stream past in such an impressive manner, there seemed little point in not taking advantage of it.

I peered through the viewfinder, concentrating on selecting the most impressive looking formations to follow. But then the neat ranks of steadily marching wildebeest began to break up. I kept the camera going and opened my left eye to see if I could spot the cause of the disturbance. The entire slope on the opposite side of the valley, which I had not been able to see in the viewfinder, was alive with movement. Everything was running. Animals poured over each crest in a torrent. I filmed for all I was worth and then reached for the binoculars.

What I was really hoping to see was another pack of dogs. A week or so earlier I had sighted a small group of 3 adults and 4 juveniles at the eastern entrance to the Angata Kiti. I had wanted to follow them for a while but hadn't dared to become diverted from the main task, that is covering the activities of Marcus and Co. But no such luck. There was no sign of a dog anywhere.

The herds settled down again. I stopped filming and sat back to watch the parade. About 10 minutes later, another panic broke out. But this time there was some focus to it. Lines of animals streamed and snaked their way along the contours. Herds of them ran, bucking and twisting, intent on escaping from some danger that seemed centred on a small kopje about 2 miles from our own ridge. I picked up the binoculars, stood up in the hatch and steadied them on the camera mount, slowly rotating it towards the open space around the kopje. When I had it lined up with the right spot I put my eyes to the glasses. Two small, dark figures stood out clearly against the bright green background and the right hand one of the pair appeared to be clubbing something to death.

I couldn't actually see what they had on the ground but it wasn't difficult to draw conclusions . . . although whether they were the right ones or not remained to be seen. But it certainly looked as if, hiding in the kopje, they had fired off an arrow, had hit a gazelle and had just rushed out to finish it off. I kept my eyes on the action. I could make out what appeared to be a spear stuck in the ground. One figure stood, holding up what looked like the legs of a gazelle. Something glinted.

At last, whatever it was they were doing was finished and they walked off to the kopje. For about a minute or so they stayed there and then they started out towards us. Before long they grew big enough in the glasses to confirm what I had already suspected. The were Maasai.

My problem was what to do next. I had no wish to become involved in a situation that was really none of my business. I was in the area to film hunting dogs and, provided no one interfered with my work, I had no intention of upsetting whatever private pleasures the Maasai might be engaged in. Large-scale poaching is, of course, the bane of conservationists in East Africa and

I too disliked the cruelty involved. But I was only too well aware that within sight of our camp stood the great rock the Maasai called Nasera. Remains excavated from beneath its overhang indicate that the site has been occupied by hunter-gatherers as far back as the Stone Age. The scene I had just witnessed was far less alien to the plains around Lemuta than I was, and it was not, if I understood matters correctly, a commercial operation but more likely an act designed to fill someone's stomach.

In the end I decided that the best thing to do under the circumstances was to show myself early on in the game to give the Maasai a chance to alter course if they wanted to avoid me for any reason. Even more to the point, I didn't want them to come up on the ridge and discover the den. There could be little doubt as to its ultimate fate if that happened. So we drove off down the ridge, away from the slope occupied by the lioness and the dogs and headed for the opposite side of the valley. There we stopped and I had another look at them. Now, though, they looked more like boys than men. They walked up to a shape I hadn't noticed lying on the ground before, and around which vultures sat. They inspected it briefly and then moved on, this time in the direction of the donkey. I had forgotten the lioness until this moment. But now, as I turned my attention back to the ridge, I saw her sneaking off just below the point at which we had been sitting. Four black dots not far behind her showed that the dogs were making sure she kept going.

The two Maasai walked up to the donkey. They stood beside the remains for quite some time, no doubt discussing its demise and wondering what its owner would have to say when told of its fate. They walked off in the direction of the Gols and disappeared. The lion having departed, what I now wanted to do was go back to the dogs. But this was something I didn't dare attempt until I was certain the Maasai had pushed off for good. So I compromised. The donkey was now attracting the attention of numerous vultures and since I needed to get good slow motion material on vultures landing for use in *Hunters*, I returned to the donkey and started filming the various species that were fast dropping out of the sky in squadrons.

Thank goodness I did, I hadn't been there more than a very few minutes when the Maasai reappeared. They marched back over the crest and stood by the car – fortunately out of sight of the den. For a minute or so they stood there saying nothing. It is not considered polite amongst the Maasai for children of that age to speak first when meeting their elders. After a suitable length of time had passed David asked them what they wanted. Their reply didn't mean much to either of us since they didn't speak Swahili. But we could understand one word and that was *Punda* meaning donkey, and it was fairly obvious from their gestures that they were out looking for the missing donkey, or was it a brace of donkeys? Throughout the morning we had heard the braying of what sounded like a young donkey coming from amongst the wildebeest. We thought we had even spotted it from time to time and so we indicated the general direction in which the two Maasai should look. Very soon they departed.

I wondered how the two boys planned to capture their quarry. Given the task of catching a donkey under similar circumstances I wouldn't have had a clue how to go about it. And from what I could see of what went on next, neither did they. When, at last, they spotted the donkey they ran towards it, waving their arms and whistling loudly. No doubt there was some good reason for doing this but it certainly wasn't obvious to me. The donkey didn't seem to catch on either. For over an hour the two Maasai performed their wild manoeuvres around us. But not once did they come within 100 yards of that donkey. I wish I could report that their antics were amusing. David thought they were hilarious. All I can say about them was that they effectively cleared out of a very considerable area, all traces of wildebeest, gazelle and every other living thing. Try as I might, I could see nothing amusing about that whatsoever.

Finally, the two boys stopped running around and sat down.

Even if they hadn't managed to get their message across to the donkey, he had undoubtedly given them a thing or two to think about. After a while the two figures rose and separated. One headed off across country, bound, presumably, to fetch reinforcements. The other strolled off to keep track of the donkey until his friend returned.

We waited for a respectable interval and then drove over to the kopje. The animal I had seen them with that morning was a wildebeest. Not much was left of it. Already the vultures had made a fair start at cleaning it up. One thing was noticeable though. There was no skin. I went over to the kopje and looked at the ground by the rock where one of them had been sitting. It was covered in wildebeest hairs. No doubt if I had looked around I would have found the skin, but evidence of poaching was the last thing I wanted.

We drove off back to the den. On the way we passed the carcass the Maasai had noticed earlier on. It was another wildebeest. Although it was pretty far gone it hadn't breathed its last. Around it circled a young calf, reluctant to leave the mother without who's support it would surely die itself. Vultures still waited in the background.

I had a close look at the animal to see if there were any signs of an arrow wound but could find nothing. Even so my feeling was that both wildebeest had probably been killed by poisoned arrows. The strange panics amongst the herds could well have been caused by the struggles of the dying animals. I wouldn't have minded betting that if we looked around a little we'd have found at least another one or two corpses.

At about 4 o'clock that afternoon, the reinforcements showed up. More Maasai, and with them two more donkeys. At about 5.30 the two sides met. Fortunately for me, the original target had wandered far away from the den and they didn't come anywhere near us. I was able to see what went on very well though. The Maasai formed up behind their donkeys and off they went at a run, using a strange gliding step which I'd read about but had never seen before. Presently, one broke away from the group and began to run after the stray in earnest. I have never seen a human being run so fast and so far. Clouds of dust rose all around the horizon as wildebeest nowhere near the actual chase became involved in the general atmosphere of unease and began running themselves. For as far as I could see Maasai were running, until they finally disappeared from view behind the far end of our ridge. David said he thought they were keeping the donkey moving so as to tire it. 'Donkey lie down when it get dark,' he explained. 'If tired then they catch him.' As it turned out we never did see the end of the performance for it grew dark and we returned to camp. I am pretty sure they got it in the end.

The next day several groups of Maasai passed along the valley. None of them came anywhere near us but I had no doubt it was the lioness they were searching for. But then, in the afternoon, fortunately while we were up on the ridge away from the den, we saw a party of Maasai approaching. We moved out towards them so that they should have no reason to cross the ridge and see what was on the other side. For a while we all stood around and looked at each other. Then we were questioned. Where did we come from? What were we doing? Where was our camp? When they learned this was near Nasera, they wanted to know if we were going to dig there. Not many months before, a party of archaeologists from Ngorongoro had come to dig under the overhang and the Maasai were curious to know the purpose of this work. Then came our turn. 'Where do you come from?' 'What are you doing?' They had been looking for the lioness all right but said they hadn't found her. I asked them about other predators . . . cheetah . . . hunting dogs. . . . 'Were there many leopard around ?' 'A few,' came the reply, 'but they are cruel to us. Sometimes they kill our goats so we must be more cruel and kill them if we can.' I wondered what the Conservator might say if he could overhear the conversation, but felt it best not to pursue that line of thought any further.

Eventually, the Maasai departed. One of them had a bell strapped to his leg. Even when they were far off across the plain we could still hear its harsh note as the party strode off towards the Gols. When I was sure they really had gone, I left as well. At about 6.30 we arrived back at camp. But our troubles weren't over yet. Three Maasai were standing there with Mathenge, our cook boy. I was beginning to recognize the regular visitors to our camp but these were men I hadn't seen before. They said nothing but simply stood and watched us unload the car.

There is a myth that most Europeans cling to about the Maasai; that they are all tall, handsome men with fine Nilotic features, positively aristocratic in their appearance and bearing. In real life an awful lot of them are as pot-bellied and bandy-legged as you and I. But the man who stepped forward when we had finished had all the physical attributes we commonly ascribe to the Maasai and a few you never dreamed of. As a man, I normally pay more attention to the female face and form than I do to members of my own sex. But I must admit that this particular individual had even me impressed. He had come from his *boma* near Piaya because they had heard that some Wazungu – white men – were camped near Nasera. A Maasai man had been attacked by a lion, he said – or was it the other way around, I wondered – and the people in the boma were afraid he would die if he was not taken to hospital soon. Would I help them?

There is of course, only one possible reply to a query like that. There is no way you can, or would want to, refuse your help. But before agreeing I wanted to know a little more about what I was letting myself in for. Piaya I had heard of but never actually visited, so I had only a vague notion as to its whereabouts. 'How far is your Manyatta?' I asked. They didn't know how far their village was. 'How long had they walked to get here?' A discussion followed. 'Three or four hours,' they thought. 'Was it in the hills?' 'Yes.' 'Can I get there by car?' 'We will help you,' they replied. 'Where did they want to take him?' 'To Loliondo,' they said as one. 'There is a good hospital there.' 'How far is Liliondo?' They didn't know.

'All right,' I said, 'I'll come. We will start tomorrow morning. It will be quicker in daylight.' 'That is good,' their spokesman said, 'but it would be better if we went now because the man might die.' I was pretty certain he wouldn't. And in any event, if he was really that far gone I doubted if a bumpy ride across country would do much for him. But I would have it on my conscience for ever if he died. And in any case, the sooner I started, the sooner I would get back.

David went off to re-fuel the car. 'You'd better make me some tea and sandwiches,' I told Mathenge. 'I already did,' he replied. I transferred my tool box to the Range Rover, put some batteries in my torch and we all got into the car. The Maasai pulled the handles off their spears, laid them on the floor in the back, and, shortly after seven, we clanked off down the track that led to the den. After half a mile or so we turned right and struck out across country. The moon had not yet risen and visibility was poor. I hadn't the faintest idea where we were except that we were keeping the mass of the Gols on our right. Occasionally, directions came from behind . . . 'Left', 'Right', and sometimes both. Before long I noticed that my queries as to which way we should go began to remain unanswered. 'Ask them if they know where we are,' I told David. It is one thing to know your way across the plains on foot, but when you are imprisoned behind the headlights of a car it isn't so easy. David held a brief conversation with the occupants of the rear seat. 'It isn't that they don't know where they are,' he reported, 'but they are all car sick'.

I pulled up. Everyone got out. It was time we stretched our legs anyway, and since it was now long past supper time I was feeling hungry. I took a corner off one of my sandwiches and drank some tea. Nearby the Maasai were all vomiting softly. I put my supper back in the box. Back we all got into the car and moved off again. Now we began to strike more bush than grassland. Frequently we had to skirt along the edges of deep *korongos* – gulleys. 'Stop!' The Maasai wanted to get out again. This time they went off a short distance and held a discussion. Plainly they were no longer as certain of their position as they had been before. Nevertheless, when they returned they were unanimous about the direction we should take. Then we began to climb. The endless herds of wildebeest through which we had been driving started to thin out and instead we passed now amongst shoals of spring hares bounding away out of the headlights. We began to stop more frequently. 'I wouldn't mind betting we're lost,' I said to David. But before he could reply a donkey brayed loudly close at hand. 'That's where our boma is,' the Maasai said. Once more we got under way. After only a short while we came to a korongo with steep and crumbling edges. I couldn't understand everything the Maasai said but there was no doubt this was a barrier we had to cross. We climbed out and walked back and forth. David got out our panga, the Maasai drew their short swords called *simis* and together they started hacking at the bush. Fortunately the soil here was very loose and this enabled me to help by heaving the worst of the boulders out of the way.

One wheel at a time I lowered the car down the dark slope. At the bottom I was convinced I would never get out again. In fact, if I had been down there in the Land Rover I don't think I would. But after some manoeuvring I managed to line up with what appeared to be a negotiable section, and, keeping my fingers well and truly crossed, gave it the gun. The Range Rover came out of the far side like a cork from a bottle. As soon as I thought I was clear I hit the brakes. The car was submerged in a dense cloud of dust. When it cleared, to my relief, the way ahead was smooth and grassy. David and the Maasai came scrambling up the slope and in another 10 minutes we were there.

It was nearly midnight when we reached our destination. The moon was up and in its light I could see people hurrying towards us, not just from one boma but several. Most of the men appeared to be *moran* – young warriors. They were remarkably silent. On each forehead gleamed the silver ornament they use to tie the braids of their hair together. The uniformity of their dress and the stylized grouping of the warriors as they stood about us seemed utterly mediaeval. Our guides came up, said 'Goodbye' and then departed. Several older men then approached and one of them spoke to me. I couldn't understand a word he said.

'First he say they want thank you for coming,' David translated.

'Now he say they give you goat for present.'

'Thank him for me please and ask him if they will keep the goat until we return.'

A lengthy discussion ensued. 'He say they bring goat to camp tomorrow,' David told me. I guessed that he had decided the offer of the goat was too good to pass up.

'He say they want us to take this man to Loliondo. Not to Ngorongoro. Doctor at Loliondo very good,' David went on.

This was Dr Wachtsinger, almost a legend in this part of Maasailand.

'Alright,' I said.

'Now he want to know if you want money for petrol.'

'No.'

At this, the old man and several moran came forward and one by one they shook me by the hand. They asked if I would wait while they fetched the man's father from a nearby boma as he was to accompany us to Loliondo. After that the gathering started to break up and things became less formal. A crowd peered into the car. Several times I felt myself touched by people who, I don't doubt, had never been this close to a European before and couldn't resist the temptation to make sure he really was flesh and bone.

After about an hour, all was ready. The injured man was led out, walking, but supported on either side. In the moonlight it was impossible to make out the extent of his injuries. They got him into the back sitting position and then four other Maasai crammed themselves in as well. One sat in the luggage compartment. The usual collection of spears and other assorted weapons of war was stowed away on the floor.

This time, unlike the first leg of the journey, our passengers were not moran but elders, and now a constant stream of advice flowed from the back. 'Faster'. . . 'Slower'. . . 'Go back'. . . 'Forward' . . . 'Turn left' . . . 'Now right' . . . one of them even knew a few words of English. 'Lefti wheeli' he kept saying.

We made our way down the hill again and out onto the plains. I maintained as smooth a course as I could to avoid too much discomfort for the injured man in the back. But every time I moved to go round a bush or a rock or a piece of rough ground, a chorus of contradictory instructions streamed from the rear. Before long any goodwill I might ever have harboured for the Maasai as a tribe had evaporated into the night air. I could cheerfully have throttled Lefti Wheeli and fed him to a passing hyena, of which not a few were to be seen patrolling the plains all around.

After what seemed like an eternity, the track left the grassland and entered bush country once more. The going became rougher. It seemed clear that the track we were on had not been used by any vehicle for some considerable length of time. I stopped. 'Are you sure this is the road to Loliondo?' David turned to the men in the back. There was no need to translate what they said. Indignation is a universally understood emotion.

We lurched on for another 10 minutes or so. Finally we arrived in a river bed. Boulders and tree trunks were strewn on all sides, as if some lunatic giant had passed that way. There was no exit on the far bank. Indeed, it was going to take some fancy manoeuvring even to retreat the way we had come. A canopy of branches hung overhead in which our lights were trapped, and I had the uncomfortable feeling that we were stuck in a vast spider's web whose owner might appear at any moment. We all got out and started moving rocks. It was very muddy. Plainly, the flash flood that had wrought the devastation had not long past and knowing the terrifying speed at which these things can develop I wanted to get out of it as soon as possible. Another one might be coming. There was no doubt that something of the sort must have been going through the minds of my Maasai friends as well for they set to work with a will and even Lefti Wheeli laboured in silence.

At last we extricated ourselves and began to retrace our tracks. I watched carefully for a turn-off we might have missed. As we drove, I began to wonder just how much further Loliondo might be. Shortly before leaving Tanzania the Range Rover speedometer had packed up. In the process of repairing it, the workshop had managed to ensure that the mileage counter now failed to operate. The fuel gauge wasn't up to much either. It would indicate 'full' for what seemed like an age. But when it did make up its mind to move you'd find yourself short of petrol faster than is funny. V8 engines are notoriously thirsty at the sort of speeds at which I had been travelling. I began to worry about the fuel situation. Then I let my thoughts run on a little further and suddenly it was as if a cold hand had slapped itself on my stomach. 'What is it today?' I asked David. He thought for a while and so did I. When you're camping out and filming, the days of the week don't mean much. 'Sunday?' he said.

During a recent fuel crisis, Tanzania had introduced a ruling under which it was forbidden to sell fuel on Saturday and to drive at all after 2 o'clock on Sunday. If it really was the weekend, and I was pretty certain it was, that meant we wouldn't be able to buy fuel in Loliondo. If we came to the notice of the police there we would be unable to drive out again. Not the happiest of prospects.

'Tell them,' I said to David, 'tell them we'll go back to camp, have some tea, fill up with fuel and then I'll take them to Ngorongoro.'

'I don't think he gonna like that,' answered David. 'They say the Government Dispensary at Ngorongoro is very bad. If we don't go to Loliondo that man he gonna die.'

'Well,' I explained, 'we've got two alternatives. Either we can stop now and wait until it gets light: try to find the Loliondo road and hope that when we do we've got enough fuel to reach Loliondo, or we can go back to camp, fill up and decide what to do at that point. And I don't give a damn what they think about it. I'm going back to camp'.

David explained to the Maasai. 'But this is the very spot,' they cried. 'Stop here and we'll show you the way. We know where we are now!'

It was a story I had heard before, I am afraid. I was so fed up with driving round in what seemed like circles that the Queen of Sheba herself could have asked me to stop and I wouldn't have given her a lift. I was tired and hungry and fed up. I didn't know where we were. I had no real idea how much fuel we had left. Moreover, for the last few hours the accompaniment of Maasai voices had hardly ceased for one moment. What they were talking about I didn't know and, quite frankly, I didn't care. But whatever it was I couldn't put up with any more of it. A glum silence reigned for the rest of the way. I found my own way back across the plains and at 6 o'clock that morning, much to Mathenge's surprise, we rolled back into camp. We all got out. The injured man was wrapped in his blanket and lay on the ground as if dead.

'First we will make some tea and have something to eat and then I will clean his wounds and we will decide what to do,' I announced. Just for once no one disagreed with me.

While the water was being boiled I went over to the wounded man. All this time I hadn't had the chance to look at him and now that I did I could see why they wanted to get to Loliondo and not to the Ngorongoro dispensary. In fact, I think he had probably got off pretty lightly. His wounds looked horrible but were really only 'superficial' when I considered what the lion could have done to him. He had cuts in his scalp that had gone through to his skull. There were deep slashes on his left thigh. And it looked as if the lion must have gripped him by the arms and shaken him, for both his forearms had been broken and his hands and arms had been bitten and scratched.

The Maasai are really quite good at diagnosing breaks and setting them. Instead of using a conventional splint or cast, they wrap a piece of animal skin around the affected part. This sets hard and sorts things out very well except when they wrap the skin around a wound as well. The ancient habit of smearing cow dung over it doesn't help much either. Under this treatment the man's right hand had begun to swell badly. I cleaned him up as best I could and then covered each of the open wounds with antiseptic cream in the hope that this would at least prevent the flies from getting to work. We then gave him a mug of hot tea and I fetched a thick pad of foam rubber on which he could rest his arms at a convenient angle. By this time he had perked up considerably and had even begun to talk and smile again. Throughout the entire journey, which at times must have been very uncomfortable indeed, the only other sound I heard from him to indicate that he was suffering was an occasional sharp intake of breath.

In daylight the journey wasn't difficult. We found where we had made the original mistake and it was exactly where Lefti Wheeli said it was. But Loliondo was much further on than I had thought – only 16 miles from the Kenya border, in fact. We'd never have made it on the one tank of fuel after first climbing up into the Gols. So at least I had the consolation of being right, even if not quite for the reason I'd originally had in mind.

We reached the Loliondo Hospital at 1 o'clock. The good Dr Wachtsinger came out, examined his new patient, and handed him over to the sisters to clean up. While that was going on he took me off to have lunch. The green lawns, the white paint, the neatness and order after the mud and shambles of the last few

Violet Mary taught me a great deal about filming cheetah.

Violet Mary on a Thomson's gazelle kill at Amboseli.

Find a cheetah with cubs and you know she's got to hunt within a limited area.

Zebra are particularly wary of lions and always approach waterholes with great caution.

Mishaps and Maasai

days made it seem as if I had suddenly been released from a lunatic asylum. 'I'm always telling them not to treat breaks like that if there's a wound underneath,' said the doctor, 'but they never listen. And those wounds aren't 3 days old like they say. It has to have happened at least 10 days ago for them to be in that condition. And if it happened all that time ago why didn't they bring him to me in Piaya? I was there last Tuesday.'

We swapped tales and I caught up with the latest news. But then it was time to go if we were to get back to camp before dark. We made it uneventfully except for a puncture. As I drove by the den, Marcus and Co. were just trotting home after their evening session. Clearly we had missed an early hunt in good light. It was irritating to have this fact pointed out in such an obvious manner. But if you let yourself get upset about such things while wildlife filming in Africa you soon develop a set of ulcers beside which that Maasai's wounds would look like scratches. So I concentrated on thinking about how comfortable my bed was going to be and pushed on towards camp.

The Maasai's chances of survival would have been pretty slim if he hadn't received medical attention at that stage. In remote areas of this kind you frequently receive requests for help from the local inhabitants. To most of them though you have to turn a deaf ear. Of course, you would like nothing more than to drive one of the elder's wives 80 miles to visit her sick mother. But in the first place you are there to film and not to run a taxi service, and in the second there is always the faint suspicion that the heart-breaking tale of woe with which you are currently being belaboured is little more than a stratagem designed to achieve some quite different end.

The mistake I made, of course, was in letting myself be talked into setting off at night. The long drive into the Gols, our meanderings across the plains and subsequent return to camp, all these had seriously depleted the stock of fuel Inky had so generously lent me only a few days before. Clearly, the sensible thing to do before starting to film again was to go to Ngorongoro straight away, taking both cars, fill up two 44 gallon drums, send David back to camp with one and drive to Ndutu myself to drop off Inky's replacement.

So, the following day, David and I resumed our travels. All went well until we reached the foot of Ngorongoro and started on the long climb up to the Conservation Area Headquarters. At that point, the generator mounting-bracket on the Land Rover broke. It was one repair I wasn't equipped to deal with. Perhaps, I thought, I should also carry welding gear. We secured the generator itself with string and some wire I had in my toolbox and pressed on. Before long, though, the Land Rover boiled. Using that system there was no means of tightening up the fanbelt properly. I got the tow rope out and we were soon under way again. I soon found that I could tow the Land Rover over the good stretches of road faster than it would climb under its own power. The trouble was that the good stretches were few and far between.

Around the Mlanje Depression it looked as if there had been an earth tremor. A long jagged crack, for all the world like the expression of dismay on Andy Capp's face when he's just had one put over on him by his mother-in-law, zigzagged along the track. It was about 18 inches wide and perhaps 3 feet deep. Woe betide any vehicle that ended up in that.

Pretty soon the road became impassable and we reached a point at which traffic had been forced to leave the normal route and plunge down into the depression itself. It was here that the Land Rover ran over the tow rope for the first time. With much cursing and swearing as the frayed ends of wire cut into our hands we got out of that tangle and resumed our journey. Three more times the cable either parted or wrapped itself round some part of the machinery. Three more times we disengaged ourselves and then, at last, we were there.

First we drove to the Tanzania Tours workshop and explained the generator problem. Very obligingly they set about welding the bracket right away. Then leaving David to keep an eye on things and bring the Land Rover to the petrol station when it was ready, I went off to start on the re-fuelling process. I reached the pump at 2.30, but there was no power. This was something I had forgotten to include in my calculations. Just in case any of you are, at this moment, planning a similar operation, I can tell you that, pumping by hand, it takes 3 hours flat to fill two 44 gallon drums, 6 jerricans, a Land Rover and a Range Rover. And it's damn tiring. So after it was over and we had made a trip to the shop to buy food, what I was really looking forward to was a quiet stop by the roadside for a cup of tea. Neither of us had had anything to eat since breakfast.

David went ahead. We drove out from the shop, turned sharp left, over the cross roads and then sharp right. I could hardly believe my eyes, but unless I was very much mistaken something fairly disastrous was about to happen to the Land Rover. Desperately, I leaned on the horn. David pulled up, looked back and stopped. I walked up to him. 'Is something the matter?' he asked. It was one of the few occasions I can remember when I got my punch line in on cue. 'Yes', I replied, 'one of your front wheels has just fallen off.'

I always carry four jacks in the Land Rover: the inadequate little thing Rover supply with the vehicle, a Tanganyika jack, a hydraulic jack, and Hi-lift. By using a combination of these we eventually managed to get the car safely propped up. As far as I could see, the split pin on the end of the half-shaft had sheared and the whole hub, plus wheel, had parted company with the car. Still, at least there was one thing to be said for it. We were lucky it hadn't chosen to come off while we were careering across the plains in hot pursuit of the dogs. Under those circumstances I don't doubt we'd have somersaulted.

Now, though, all I could do was stand and gaze in dismay at the mess inside. As far as I could see it could not be repaired without spares which I just didn't have. Moreover, to make things worse it was getting dark and the temperature, since we were at 9,000 feet, was dropping rapidly. It looked as if we were in for an uncomfortable night. But rather than resign myself to this at quite such an early stage in the game I got out one of the jerricans and we made a start on cleaning out the drum, separating the wheel from the hub and generally tidying things up. Once everything was clean, I thought, things might look better. They didn't. I tried getting the castle nut onto the end of the half-shaft but it wouldn't take more than a turn and a half before it jammed. The thread didn't look too bad, though, so I set about using the nut as a die to clear it out. In any event, spares or no spares, there was nothing we could do until that matter had been set to rights, so I began to turn the nut back and forth, forcing it a fraction further with each swing. Back and forth. Back and forth. At this rate it was going to take all night. But at least it was something to do. Something with some purpose in it. And, what's more, something to keep me warm.

Various groups of locals passed by. Each one stopped to view the catastrophe, offer their regrets and, naturally, give advice. I left David to deal with the diplomacy and continued turning the nut. Finally a car pulled up. In it was Mr Marua from Ngorongoro Conservation Area Headquarters. I explained what had happened. He turned and said something to his passenger. When he jumped out, I saw it was the mechanic from the workshop who had repaired the generator bracket earlier on. He crossed to the car and examined the remains. 'No problem,' he said. 'Wait there and I'll be back in a minute.' They drove away to fetch spares from the workshop.

By 9.30, quite incredibly, we were on the road again, heading towards Seronera. I owed that mechanic much more than the money he refused to take for his work, and even though I could see it was impossible to get to Ndutu that night, who cared? We were moving again.

Slowly now, for we were heavily loaded, we made our way down the track leading back onto the plains. Once we were off the hill conditions improved, but the euphoria that had stemmed from our unexpected deliverance had at last worn off and I was beginning to feel tired. My eyes felt like a couple of lead ballons. Twice the car almost lurched off the road, but the thought of my bed and a hot drink back at camp kept me going. At last we reached the pile of stones that marked the turn off to Loliondo. I had been relying on the moon to illuminate Lemuta Hill without which crossing the plains on anything like a straight line at night is impossible. We were so late now that the moon had almost set. I was determined to keep going. I calculated that we needed to travel for about 30 minutes from the turn-off at which point, if I turned 90 degrees right, I ought to see Lemuta against the sky. So, after half an hour, I turned and switched off the lights to let my eyes grow accustomed to the dark. I peered out. Nothing. Moreover it was beginning to get misty. Since I had learned the futility of driving around on the plains in the dark only a couple of nights ago there seemed little point in making an idiot of myself all over again. There was nothing for it but to stop where I was.

When David came up in the Land Rover we parked side by side and settled down to sleep. It was then two-thirty. I couldn't honestly claim that the next 3 hours were the most uncomfortable I've ever spent, but they came close to it. I had had the rear seat of the Range Rover folded forward so that the 44 gallon drum wasn't sitting over the rear springs. The passenger side in front was piled high with odds and ends, so I had no option but to sit up and rest my head on the steering wheel. I didn't sleep much. When dawn came I woke David, we warmed the engines, and started off again.

As soon as we came up onto a ridge from which we could actually see Nasera and the entrance to the Angata Kiti, I left David to go on alone and turned back towards Ndutu. The thought of breakfast, a hot shower and a shave hastened me on my way. The causeway was still flooded and while driving around the detour I got stuck in the mud again, but by 11 o'clock I was in the lodge dining room at Ndutu eating breakfast. True, there were no showers as the water pump was 'kaput', but since everyone was going to SRI for a film show that evening, and at Seronera you could actually get a hot bath, even this set-back no longer seemed a disappointment. I would go to Seronera with them. What was one more day out of my filming schedule after the events of the last 48 hours?

Next day, I finally got back to work. As we drove over the crest of the ridge once more, I kept my fingers well and truly crossed. Any number of things could have happened to the den. It is true there weren't many hyena around, but the pack's rather casual attitude towards them always worried me. I constantly dreaded the possibility that one day, returning from a hunt, we might see a hyena actually at the den. Nor was I all that easy in my mind about the reaction of the local Maasai towards a litter of pups. I simply couldn't believe that, given the opportunity, they would pass up the chance to slaughter them. But no, there they all were, stretched out around the den as usual. Marcus half lifted his head and glanced at the car as we approached. The others didn't even bother to do that. There was of course no way of telling just what golden opportunities had been missed through the recent cycle of disasters that had overtaken me. But that was something I didn't want to know about. The main thing was that we were back, still in one piece, all stocked up and once again ready to go.

6
Kali's Litter

So far I haven't said much about Kali's litter of thirteen puppies. In fact it was quite a long time before I was even sure how many there were. Initially, they spent all their time below ground. But even when they did appear it seemed to me they responded only to a very limited number of signals. When one reacted, they all did. So either you had no pups in sight or you had the lot. Counting them as the avalanche hurtled back and forth was no easy task. Eventually things settled down a bit. Pups became more venturesome. The mass split up and individuals started to wander about exploring their environment, carrying pieces of grass and twig around, tumbling in and out of the burrow and spreading out so that instead of reaching a different answer every time I counted, the figure thirteen began to come up with some regularity. And in the end, thirteen it was, two of them females.

The biggest threat to young puppies as yet unable to leave the burrow almost certainly lies in the spotted hyena. The dogs seem to realize this and, when they have a den, behave towards hyena in a most aggressive manner, running at them from a considerable distance. I have never heard of them killing one, and I don't think it would ever come to that, but they certainly give the hyena a very rough time while they are about it. Their unfortunate victim has only one defence and that is to run for the nearest hole, in which it then squats in order to protect its rear end. Once in that position the hyena twists and turns its body, its mouth wide open, making clumsy lunges at its assailants. But while it is warding off the dogs in front, others dart in and tear at its skin from behind. By the time that they get tired of this game, what they leave behind is usually a very tatty looking hyena indeed.

Although I saw the Genghis Pack chase hyenas on a number of occasions, they did so only in a very half-hearted manner and I was never able to get film of this type of interaction, something that I had more or less taken for granted. It seemed that if I wanted it badly enough I would have to look for it elsewhere.

If they had denned in the vicinity of Naabi or on the Mara River and had adopted a similar attitude towards the far more numerous hyenas that patrolled in those areas, I doubt if their puppies would have survived for long. I suspect, though, that under these circumstances their approach to the problem would have been a lot different. Instead of leaving the den to hunt with the pack, Kali would have been forced to spend much more time at home guarding her offspring.

One day they met and chased a hyena while out hunting. Immediately after that encounter Kali turned and made for the burrow, where she went straight underground and didn't reappear, even though, at that stage, the dogs hadn't killed. So she must have been hungry. It was almost as if the sight of the hyena had made her realize the risk she was running in leaving her young unguarded.

I hope I haven't created the impression that Kali wasn't a good mother or that the Genghis Pack males weren't very competent at looking after their young. It was simply that the dog/hyena interactions which had been a daily feature of life in the two packs I had filmed prior to this assignment had provided really good material. As a cameraman, I was disappointed not to get these scenes again. But from the other point of view I was delighted there were so few hyena around. This lack of rival predators meant that the pups' chances of survival were greatly increased.

Kali's Litter

I had also been hoping I might get a sequence on the dogs moving dens. Normally, this happens several times before the pups are old enough to travel with the pack. When they are very small their mother usually carries some of them in the moving process. This is quite common amongst predators. Cheetah, lion and hyena all carry their young. I've even seen mongoose doing so at times. The reason why a dog carrying its young makes such good film is that the bitch picks up the pups by gripping them round the head. I've seen a female carrying young with the wretched infant's head right inside her mouth. The pup's hind legs are running like mad, usually either in contact with the ground or just above it. To the human onlooker this is very amusing indeed, although I don't doubt that the pup sees it in quite a different light. Unfortunately for me, the Genghis Pack den consisted of an absolute maze of burrows, so there was no incentive for Kali to move very far. She certainly carried her young all right. If they found their way into a burrow she didn't approve of she'd dive in and emerge with a wriggling mouthful which she would then deposit back in the right hole. I even saw Marcus at it as well. From a film stand-point this wasn't very satisfactory. What you want is a fairly protracted movement. If the distance between dens is 30 or 40 yards, you can give the audience a good look at what's going on. But if the dog dives into a burrow, grabs a pup, hauls it out and straightaway drops it into another one, all within the space of a few seconds, you almost have to say to the audience, 'Now watch carefully. Something interesting is going to happen.' While this sort of thing may be acceptable for home movies, it is not really what television is all about.

Within the cocoon provided for them by hunting dog society, the puppies lead a reasonably secure existence. Guarded against marauding hyena while the pack is away about its work, escorted from burrow to burrow, they probably stand a better chance of surviving the first few vulnerable weeks than do the young of most predators. At this stage, too, the young dogs start learning the strange language of co-operation. To gain the benefits that derive from a social existence, the puppies must pay a price for acceptance in the club. They must learn to read the signals, to respond in kind, to sublimate the aggressive instincts without which no predator can hope to survive, to draw, as individuals, on the strengths of the pack. And yet, in spite of the care apparently lavished upon them and the rapidity with which their integration within the social framework of the group occurs, it is exceptional for more than two or three of the puppies to survive to reach adulthood.

In order to ensure a stable population, all that a pair of dogs needs to do is raise to maturity two of their young to replace themselves by the time they die. If you assume that the average life span of a hunting dog is 10 years and that for 8 of these the female is capable of producing at least 10 pups per year, then, in theory, out of the 80 pups to which she gives birth, no fewer than 78 can die without it being a disaster. But a unit of 2 dogs hunting alone isn't very efficient and as such would be unlikely to survive. So in practice what the two need to do is rear perhaps 4 or 5 of their offspring. But even if you put this as high as 10, then 70 out of 80 are still going to die. On the face of it, seems a rather wasteful system. But is it?

If every pup born survived, in next to no time you would be able to walk across the Serengeti on the backs of hunting dogs. On the other hand, if no pups survived the dogs would rapidly become extinct. Somewhere in between these two extremes lies the correct solution in terms of numbers. But numbers aren't everything. What is equally needed is the right number of the right type, and I don't just mean males and females. A predator needs to possess certain physical characteristics – speed, stamina, hunting skill. It also needs to be aggressive. And what the dogs are doing by producing so many pups is simply setting up the competitive environment within which any individual with the attributes essential to survival will be able to display them. In fact, I would go so far as to say I think it may even be advantageous if, at some stage during the first 12 months of the puppies' existence, before they've developed the capacity to support themselves, food should become short. When that happens the pup that wins through will be the one who learns quickly, adapts to the changed situation and is strong enough and determined enough to seize whatever food it requires at the expense of its litter mates.

If the dogs produced fewer puppies some might slip through the net which didn't really deserve to. It is important, vital even, that no dog lives which one day might be in a position to perpetuate some undesirable characteristic. This system may not lead to the development of a more intelligent dog, but it certainly ensures that those individuals that do survive possess desirable physical characteristics and at least enough intelligence to carry the species through to the next generation. So if you were to say to me 'Ten puppies out of eighty doesn't sound as if the dogs are very successful,' I'd have to disagree. On the contrary, 10 pups out of 80 is highly successful. It means that the system is working. The others were weighed in the balance, found wanting and disposed of before they could become a burden on society. The system is there to detect such shortcomings before they can be bred into the pack. Once detected they are dealt with in the time-honoured fashion.

All this is no more than theory of course, the sort of thing that goes through your mind when you sit watching and filming puppies playing happily around the den and realize what trials lie in store for them.

Only by maintaining records over a lengthy period is it possible to gain some idea whether or not what seems like a reasonable probability in theory is actually being borne out in practice. It is an indication of the effort that needs to be maintained in a park such as the Serengeti if the authorities are at least to be aware of the trends prevailing amongst the animal populations living in the area under their control. Hunting dogs are an endangered species. Most people realize this. But it isn't enough to sit and bemoan the fact. Once you accept responsibility for the management of an area within which endangered species exist, my belief is that you also accept the need at least to monitor their status. In this case, records did exist. Since 1968, out of 70 pups known to have been born into the Genghis Pack only one, Marcus, had survived. A similar state of affairs was known to prevail amongst the other plains packs. No one knows of course, whether the dogs concerned are suffering a drastic decline or whether this is no more than a temporary hiccup. Plotted on a 10 year time base it doesn't look good. Over 1,000 years?

What did seem to me disturbing was the fact that at the end of 1977 all the SRI scientists working on dogs were due to leave and at that point hunting dogs would be no one's special interest. No discredit to the excellent people concerned but this short-term interest strikes me as a general weakness of scientific work in the field. A dedicated worker completes his thesis or maybe his grant runs out. He moves on. Again, if he or she is ambitious they may wish to take on some other study, perhaps in another country, another continent. And so the dogs, rhino, giraffe or whatever which have been temporarily of burning scientific interest are left unstudied, perhaps for a long time.

Even when there were scientists on the Serengeti actively attempting to keep track of the plains packs, the Genghis Pack, for example, was hardly seen at all during 1976. And it was sheer luck, as I've already recounted, that they were found by Inky in 1977. But when no one is left to keep track of what's going on, what will happen? The Genghis Pack could be wiped out by disease, starvation, or a fight with another group and this could easily happen without anyone knowing about it. I suppose eventually people would be going around saying, 'It's strange, we don't seem to see hunting dogs as often as we used to,' and it is not completely impossible to believe that in the end no dogs will be seen at all.

But even if we knew what was going on, are we able to do

anything about it? Personally I'm not one of those people who believe that because an animal appears to be in difficulties we have to jump in with both feet and try to help it immediately. All too often the basic information doesn't exist which permits action of this kind to be taken without doing more harm than good. But I think you can reasonably say that if a watch is being kept on an endangered species and it is appreciated that it is getting into difficulties, then at least the possibility exists that the people concerned will come up with ideas as to the root cause of the problem. In that case there would be a *chance* something could be done.

True, my prime task was to help make a television Special in which hunting dogs would play a star part. But in shooting, perhaps over-shooting film on the dogs, I know that I hoped I would be able to contribute something to the total knowledge of the species and in this I had the full approval of *Survival*. I intended to have all my scenes scrutinized and analyzed by those scientists still working on the species, even if the finer points of behaviour recorded by my camera did not find their way into the finished film.

Despite my admiration for hunting dogs in general and the Genghis Pack in particular, their daily round of activities more often than not resulted in some fairly hair-raising sights.

On 23 May for instance, we followed the dogs away from the den on their evening hunt but soon lost contact with them when they dashed into the midst of a great mob of wildebeest. Clouds of dust rose into the air and visibility fell to a few yards within a matter of seconds. I filmed what I could and then we joined on to one side of a column of animals galloping off in what I took to be the general direction of Lemuta. Unfortunately, we were on the down-wind side of the hunt and soon became enveloped in a choking cloud of dust. Since there was an obvious danger that we might drive full tilt into a hyena hole, I shouted to David to turn right and try to get on the other side of the stampede where we might at least see something of what was going on. Just as we emerged from the cloud, Marcus shot across our bows, hard on the heels of a solitary calf. Just a few yards beyond him Homer had singled out his own victim and I could see Kali there too. They ran their quarry to a standstill and while Homer gripped its throat to immobilize it, Kali attacked its left hand side just in front of the hind leg. She quickly opened up a hole and through this the contents of its stomach began to fall out. Pretty horrible, but that's the way dogs kill. Then Jinja joined in. But still the calf wouldn't give up. Although they had it down now and its hindquarters appeared to be connected to its front end by little more than its spinal column, it scrabbled along in the dust literally clawing its way towards the car with its front legs. When it was no more than 10 feet away though, Kali and Homer who had both been feasting on the trail of intestines the calf was dragging behind it, suddenly woke up to what was happening and the two of them pulled the intestines free.

I have done my best to keep descriptions of this sort to an absolute minimum. When filming, I tried to keep kills in long- or mid-shot, but most people are aware that hunting dogs have a very bad reputation as 'ruthless killers', and unless you have some inkling of why this should be it is difficult to understand why the dogs tend to provoke such strong views. Even people who are used to it sometimes find the killing hard to take. On one occasion when I was filming hunting dogs one of the game scouts came up to me and said 'You're very lucky to be able to film this pack.' At first I thought he was referring to the fact that they seldom settle for so long in one place as these had. But then he went on, 'Bwana X', [and he gave the name of the previous Game Warden, a much respected character in those parts] 'he couldn't stand hunting dogs. If he'd known they were here he'd have come over and shot the lot.' Well, that is certainly one way out of the situation. But whether it makes us any better than the animals we so casually blot off the face of the earth to save our own feelings, is something I'm still trying to figure out.

There is also the viewpoint that says, in effect, an animal

being killed by predators is in a state of shock and therefore largely unaware of its predicament. Personally, I have my doubts. I don't mean to say by this that they necessarily suffer to the same extent that we might under similar circumstances. Nor am I attempting to assert that shock isn't a factor to be taken into consideration. It is just that adding things up in my diary recently, and realizing that I have now been present at over 150 hunting dog kills, this just isn't the impression I retain.

When a pack of dogs seizes a gazelle or young calf – something not much bigger than they are – it all happens very quickly. The unfortunate animal is torn to pieces, usually within seconds. But with a bigger animal it's different.

The dogs we were following at the time were hunting regularly, morning and evening. There were only four of them, three males and a female, and the female, having a litter of small puppies to attend to, was not at that stage playing any part in the actual hunting activity.

At about 4.30 the three dogs that had been lying some way off from the burrow got up, stretched, and then trotted over to the female to start their 'greeting ritual'! The theory is that there is no point in living as a pack without also working as one. Accordingly, some method must be found to synchronize the movements of the group. The ceremony in which the dogs rush around in circles, shoulder to shoulder, uttering their strange bird-like calls is supposed to fulfil this role. Whether this is entirely correct or not I am by no means sure, but for the moment it is what the experts say, so let us accept it. So the males, having undertaken the prescribed greeting ritual, left the female lying with her offspring and trotted off down the valley. Wildebeest grazed in all directions, an immeasureable host of small black dots, scattered across the emerald green of the plains as far as the eye could see.

After about 10 minutes, the dogs had run a yearling wildebeest to a standstill and the now familiar tableau had formed.

One dog had the victim by the muzzle, a second gripped it high up under the throat. But the third, which we had noticed lagging behind in an entirely uncharacteristic fashion, lay down as soon as the other two stopped running and vomited. On a couple of occasions it stirred itself sufficiently to get up and bite the wildebeest on the back legs, but otherwise it took no significant role in the proceedings.

The result was a stalemate. The dogs at the front could do no more than prevent their victim running off. A couple of 40 pound dogs hanging onto your nose acts as a very effective brake. But however painful their hold, they cannot kill from that position. The damage is done, under normal circumstances, by the other members of the pack which tear at the animal's stomach, ripping at its skin until its intestines drop out and it bleeds to death.

I never really got used to watching it. It is a hard business; a dreadful way to die, and certainly there is no point in filming much of what happens for, as a photographer, you must never lose sight of the fact that people pay to be entertained and even educated, but not sickened. If the proceedings look bad in their natural context, what sort of impression are they going to create when brought into the family living room at tea-time on Sunday afternoon? Even if you film it all, the producer will wisely ask his film editor to cut the action at the point the victim goes down and before the blood starts to flow.

On this occasion, though, I was curious to see what would happen. We drew closer and stopped. It must have been a terrifying situation for the wildebeest. In all probability this was the first time in its life that it had been separated from the mass of its companions. Now it stood, literally eyeball to eyeball with a fierce predator whose teeth were sunk into its nose and whose jaws I could see contracting vigorously as they tightened into the flesh. If ever a situation existed in which 'shock' might have been expected to play a part, this was it.

But, spurred on by the presence of the vehicle, which it

clearly recognized as a possible means of salvation, the wildebeest made a last desperate effort to escape. Tearing loose from the dog at its nose, it bolted for the car. When it reached us it whirled, and, going down on its 'knees', as wildebeest often do when arguing amongst themselves, turned to face its attackers.

There was little the dogs could do about it. The wildebeest now had its rear protected by the Land Rover. Its hindquarters were jammed tightly against the door not 2 feet from my left hand. The dogs lunged at the wildebeest, their shrill growling and the force of their thrusts taking even me by surprise. I had seen many dogs in action from a range of perhaps 30 or 40 feet. Nevertheless, I was totally unprepared for the unbelievable ferocity of their attacks when witnessed from a distance of no more than a yard or so.

But their attempts to grab its nose again were unsuccessful. The wildebeest had tucked its muzzle in close to the ground. From its kneeling position it countered every move made by the dogs with its sharp, spikey little horns. It was stalemate. As long as the dogs stayed close, the wildebeest couldn't escape. As long as it didn't panic and run, there wasn't much the dogs could do either.

By this time it was six-thirty. The shadows were lengthening and I was beginning to wonder how much longer I'd have to wait. Then, suddenly, all three dogs rose and moved off. They gave no warning, and made no sign that a change of plan was imminent. As one, they simply got up and left. Their intended victim watched them go. When they were no more than 50 yards away, he too departed, settling into that strange, gliding trot used by wildebeest only in moments of extreme agitation. I held my breath, for I was sure he would be spotted, and after such a courageous defence I'd have hated to see him caught. But no, his luck held and in seconds he was swallowed up in the mass of the nearby herds. Eventually the dogs did turn and come back. One of them even got down and looked under the car. But the yearling had gone and that was that.

So there was one wildebeest that didn't lose its head in a situation in which it could certainly have been excused for doing so. It sought protection from an object it would have run from under normal circumstances. It quickly adopted the right method of defence and when the time came promptly made good its escape.

It is true that I have seen a pregnant wildebeest, chased to exhaustion, sitting motionless, head up, while several dogs took a meal from its hindquarters. I know these sort of things do happen. But most wildebeest, cornered by dogs, fight hard, and, if there is a car around, struggle desperately to reach it. Yearlings resist in an especially violent manner.

I am not claiming that wild animals have any concept of death, or anything of that sort. But within certain limits I feel they know very well what is happening to them and to suggest they do not is, in my view, a doubtful proposition to say the least of it.

As a matter of fact, the Genghis Pack's kills were, on the whole, rather less horrifying to watch than many I had seen before. When I first started filming them, Marcus didn't seem to have things entirely under control, and from his behaviour at that stage it was a lot easier to appreciate the value of the greeting ceremony by virtue of having seen the shambles that could arise when the pack neglected to use it properly. Not infrequently, Marcus would find himself out on his own and it was noticeable that without Jinja and Homer to back him up he wasn't able to cope too well. During the $2\frac{1}{2}$ months I watched them, though, he developed a method of killing on his own, and eventually I had the impression that he was able to catch a calf, pull it down, kill it and get a meal off it more rapidly than the other three combined.

Wildebeest calves bleat in a quite heart-rending manner when caught. This was something Marcus appeared to dislike. Relinquishing his hold on the rear end he would rush round and dive at the animal's throat. Considering what was going on at the time this was probably the kindest thing he could have done, although I doubt if kindness was quite what he had in mind. As a method of stopping the noise though it was fully effective. After a couple of minutes like this he would then let go and move round to the back to resume feeding again.

Then one day I saw the trio pull a calf down and Marcus went straight for the throat without bothering about the preliminaries. From that point on, whenever he was on his own, it seemed to me that he realized this was the most effective method of bringing the situation under control. He would hang onto the throat until, presumably, he felt the animal stop struggling. Only after that would he go round the back and start tearing at its belly. Occasionally the victim would regain consciousness, lift its head and look back to see what was going on. Then Marcus would dive at it again. But this didn't always happen and several times I had the impression he might have actually killed the animal by this method. Of course, no single dog is powerful enough to kill a calf that is more than, say, 4 months old. After that they are too strong and have developed a heavy fold of skin below the throat which I suspect the dogs can not penetrate. But against quite young calves this tactic was very effective. Perhaps the most telling commentary on the value of the method came when the other males, Homer and Jinja, began to copy his technique.

Inevitably, the ideal static filming situation provided by the den had to come to an end. Within a matter of days now the pack would leave the den, for the pups were now old and strong enough to accompany the adults. Every day they seemed to increase in size. As they did so, of course, so did their appetites. At the same time, though, their food supply had fallen off to a marked extent. The migration of wildebeest was moving on. On 28 May the plains has almost emptied of wildebeest and that evening all the dogs got was a gazelle. Next morning they found nothing. That evening, after a swing through territory which, until recently had yielded rich pickings with little effort, they finally pounced on a baby Thomson's gazelle. Kali actually got to it first, but, when Marcus ran up bent on grabbing the other end, she ran off, head held high, twisting and turning until he got the message and stopped. This offering she bore away to the den and dropped for her offspring.

I now set about filming the tasks I had left until last, and didn't dare delay any longer. Most urgent amongst these was a series of identification pictures, for I planned to return to the area from time to time in the hope of re-locating the pack and checking on its progress. And to this end I needed a file of stills to consult. Memory is a notoriously unreliable agent for work of this kind.

One of the differences between the Genghis Pack and others I had filmed was their observance at the kill of an order of precedence. I think I am right in saying that this seldom happens amongst hunting dogs. When they kill they feed fairly amicably alongside each other. Every dog bolts down whatever it can as rapidly as it can. But in recent years there has been a considerable increase in the number of hyenas out on the plains and it is seldom that the dogs occupy a burrow which doesn't have at least a small population of hyena resident somewhere in the vicinity. Once a pack establishes itself in their area the hyena are not slow to catch on. When they see the dogs pass they tag on to the rear of the procession. The dogs, therefore, have to gulp down as much of the meat as they can before being overwhelmed. So they normally have little time to argue over the niceties of who eats next to or before whom.

I cannot remember how many hyena I saw between Lemuta and the Gols, but no more than twenty in a period of $2\frac{1}{2}$ months. I suspect that the Maasai have something to do with this. When the area is invaded by wildebeest the Maasai move their cattle up into the Gols, for they believe the cows become infected with disease at this time. When they come down to the plains again, the herdsmen are invariably ruthless in eliminating any hyena young. So the hyena never get a chance to build up in any numbers in this area. Thus, hyena were not a factor that influenced the Genghis Pack's eating behaviour to any noticeable extent.

Marcus was usually first onto the prey. Then the others joined in. They all shared in the task of despatching their victim. While this was going on Homer and Jinja seized whatever they could and devoured it rapidly. But then, if Kali was at the kill, they stood to one side until she and Marcus had taken what they wanted. After this, Homer would eat. Jinja waited until the end of the feast, although when wildebeest were on the menu this still left him with a good meal.

Early on the morning of 30 May, the dogs came unexpectedly on a small herd of wildebeest. They brought down a calf and now, after several days of hunting gazelle, it was noticeable how things had changed. Jinja must have been very hungry because he tore into the unexpected meal with the rest of them. You could tell he was apprehensive by the position of his tail, which he held high up above the horizontal, a clear indication of his emotional state.

I filmed what was going on. Although there wasn't really enough light the dogs were on the crest of a ridge so I was able to expose for the background of sky and leave the action to appear in silhouette. If it came off, it would be a great shot, perhaps even an opening sequence for the hunting dog section of the Special. In normal film-making, the cameraman usually has a chance to view his 'rushes' within 24 hours. No such conveniences apply when you are out in the bush. So I wouldn't know for a long time how effective the scene was.

The cameraman in the field does his best to send film out for processing at regular intervals. He should then receive a cable back from head office commenting on its technical quality, its relevance to the story and so on. But I had been refused permission to do this by the Central Bank of Tanzania until the project was finished, and although I was reasonably certain this ruling was the result of a misunderstanding, I could not afford the time to go to Dar-es-Salaam and explain matters.

So from February through to the end of June I worked away without any check on what I was producing. This was worrying to say the least. Of course, there is always a communication problem in this kind of work. It cuts both ways. To most cameramen, me included, the relief at being in a position in which head office cannot get at you on a day-to-day basis is considerable. But by the same token, you make your own mistakes and so your position is somewhat exposed if things go wrong.

To me, the social life of the Genghis Pack, the relationships between the various dogs, the struggle between Marcus and Homer, were of absorbing interest. But all this manifested itself only in a series of very low-key encounters, the turn of a neck, a quick nip, a nibble at a foreleg. I filmed it all but, despite the fact that Colin Willock, the producer, and his team are highly experienced and knowledgeable wildlife film-makers, I had no way of knowing what they would make of my efforts. I could hear Colin saying 'Why the hell is he over-shooting so badly?'

Most of the day the dogs lay around and slept, or at least rested. Although casual encounters did occur during this period, most of the action took place either at the pre-hunt greeting ritual or at the kill itself, for it was only at these times that all the adult members of the group were in close contact. I couldn't afford to run the camera every time a dog walked past one of its neighbours, simply in the hope that something might happen. But I needed to capture enough significant footage to enable *Survival* at least to establish each of the dogs as a character in its own right. To do this I shot away in slow-motion whenever I felt that by doing so there was a likelihood this would provide the sort of material which would show which dog was Marcus, which was Homer, and why it was that Jinja cringed so spectacularly at Marcus' approach, while Homer didn't.

Kali's Litter

As the pups grew daily more and more independent, I couldn't wait for the pack finally to leave the den. I could then drive to Dar and ship my exposed footage.

The end was not long in coming. On 30 May at 10.30, Kali rose, shook herself, and without further ado walked off down the hill towards a patch of erosion on the next crest to which she had often gone to lie up for the day when the pups were smaller. But now they followed her. Marcus, Homer and Jinja all got up and walked off as well. Together they trotted across the valley and up the other side. At the top, the adults all sorted out comfortable places in which to rest. The pups settled separately in their own group.

They had followed the adults away from the den several times before, sometimes much further than to their present position, but each time Kali had turned round and led them back to the den. The fact that she had not done so on this occasion seemed to me to indicate they had now left their birth-place for good.

Shortly before four in the afternoon the arrival of some vultures alerted the dogs to the presence of a dead Thomson's gazelle fawn near at hand. Jinja and Kali took it apart. It was interesting to see that Marcus made no attempt to interfere with Jinja. Instead he hung around Kali with his ears pricked. Obviously he would have liked some of the meat. In the end she did leave a little behind but it was no more than a mouthful.

At about 5.15 the pack set off on their travels once again. We followed as they headed in a north-easterly direction. By 6.15 they were heading down a valley into a part of the plains I hadn't seen before. But now my fuel pump was giving trouble so I pulled up alongside the Range Rover and told the driver I intended to head back for camp in the hope that I would get there before dark.

Next morning we were up early. I took the pump off, cleaned the points and replaced it. By 9.30 we had re-located the pack. They had travelled only a few yards further the previous evening and, having killed a gazelle before daybreak, had already

Hunters of the Plains

settled down for the day. I spent the time taking more identification stills.

That evening they set out from their new den leaving the pups behind. They trotted up the eastern slope of the valley and when they went down the other side we sat on the ridge and watched them go. The country here is breathtakingly beautiful. It is far hillier. The mountains rise in the background. Great slabs of rock thrust up out of the plains. I can't describe it adequately. It looked like the promised land to me. As we sat there, the full moon rose, pink and heavy from behind a thin bank of cloud. Beneath us, fold after fold of ground, each one darker than the next, fell away into the distance. Along one of these ridges we could just make out the shapes of Marcus, Kali, Jinja, and Homer as they went on down into the depths. I watched for as long as I could, trying to fix the scene in my memory for I knew it was unlikely I would ever see anything like it again.

7
Conservation and Violet Mary

The human memory is a strange phenomenon and convenient too. From it we recall only those things of which we wish to be reminded. As old age creeps up on us, almost inevitably the past becomes a refuge against the discomforts of the present. Food was cheaper, clothes made better, and, of course, the behaviour of the young beyond comparison.

As a photographer I am constantly reminded of this. 'You should have seen this place twenty years ago,' the old hands say. 'The animals then had to be seen to be believed.' All right, I'll go for that. Why not? 'And the lions! Well, I mean, they were all over the place. Poached out now of course, but then, what can you expect!'

But how much of this sort of thing is actually true?

A strange, rather glamorous aura has built up around the 'big cats'. Everyone wants to see them and if they aren't seen then one is assured that they are on the decline. But are they?

There is no doubt that the overall number of predators in East Africa has decreased – the amount of land taken over for cultivation has seen to that – but there is little hard evidence to suggest that in many of those areas where people go to see them, in national parks and reserves, they are declining in density at any greater rate than their prey species. The fact is

Hunters of the Plains

that predators are always small in number when compared with their prey and their numbers rise and fall with the amount of prey available. Their densities have never been all that high, but because this situation is not always fully appreciated, there is a tendency amongst people who are disappointed at not seeing them to assume that, 50 years or so ago, for example, lion, leopard and cheetah could be seen sitting around under every tree. Almost certainly this is not true and the cheetah is a notable case in point.

Consider the predators in their domesticated state. It is the dog that will obey commands, can be taught tricks and is often referred to as 'man's best friend'. The cat, on the other hand, is probably behaving in much the same way as it did when it first started hanging around cave mouths scavenging for scraps. In other words, it would appear that cats in general have invested far more heavily in instinct than in adaptability. But as the land available to predators decreases year by year, so the pressure on them to adapt to changing circumstances grows more and more severe. But if survival depends on adaptability, the converse must also be true. When the heat is really on, specialization is a great handicap. In this respect the most specialized of all the animals I aimed to film for *Hunters* was the cheetah. I had hoped to find cheetah hunting in the same general area as the dogs.

The cheetah is the smallest of all the 'big cats'. About the largest animal it can kill on a regular basis is the impala. This means that its food sources are that much more limited and its dependence on a narrower range of prey species that much greater. Because it is smaller and lacks the power of the other predators, the cheetah has to eat quickly, for any of its competitors can drive it from the kill. And because it is specialized for catching small prey, in open country, almost always in daylight, it has a limited time in which to hunt. The lion and leopard have 24 hours; the cheetah has only twelve.

So, in a situation in which the land available to it is steadily shrinking, a cat that is highly specialized and lacking adaptability must be at a disadvantage.

It seems reasonable to suppose that the cheetah as we now know it evolved in conditions that resembled the flood plains of northern Kenya today. There these animals developed the mechanisms that allowed them to exist at very low population densities. There they exist to this day, probably in much the same numbers as they always have, for the dry thornbush holds little attraction for man and is likely to remain that way for some time to come.

The danger to cheetah is that through mismanagement, through a failure on the part of those concerned to appreciate their basic needs, they will disappear from those places where people now go to see them and will then be found only at very low densities in their typical primaeval habitats.

At this point, if not extinct, the cheetah could certainly be said to have 'vanished' for very few people would ever get to see one. If such a day should come to pass, it would be a sad one for the human race. Not only would a very beautiful and interesting animal have been driven from the ecological niche it now occupies amongst the company of predators still left to us, but it would also represent a failure to come to terms with a problem that presently concerns us very deeply.

Again in terms of an animal like the cheetah, the willingness to tolerate in our midst a form of life that is both aesthetically pleasing and of some economic benefit represents a small step along the road to sanity. It is by no means impossible to believe that upon such steps the fate of some future generation of our own kind may eventually depend.

Quite often the first few days of a new project turn out to be extremely frustrating. When I embarked on the opening phase of the cheetah filming, matters ran true to form and were, as it turned out, to continue doing so.

Last time I filmed a cheetah was the occasion on which I covered the adventures of Violet Mary, a cheetah who

Hunters of the Plains

subsequently became the heroine, if that is the right description to use, of a programme in a BBC-Time-Life co-production entitled *Run Cheetah Run*. I had been working in Amboseli in southern Kenya. Before leaving I gave the game scout who had been helping me a postcard to send off if and when he found either a cheetah with young cubs or, preferably, one he thought was pregnant.

This was the situation I needed in order to get a cheetah programme on the go. So, when the card finally arrived, I hurried off to Amboseli as fast as I could. Not fast enough, as it turned out. Although the cheetah had been seen the previous week, at the time I arrived on the scene she wasn't to be found anywhere. I searched the entire area, but nothing. I could have missed her of course. But as far as I was concerned I doubted this and for all practical purposes there wasn't a cheetah anywhere within 10 miles of Amboseli with anything even remotely resembling a cub. This put me in a difficult position. I had agreed to make the film. In fact, I very much wanted to make it for I felt that cheetah were a rather neglected subject. I was also afraid, that having talked my way into it, if I subsequently backed out again, it might be a long time before I got another chance . . . if ever.

So, before throwing in the towel, I decided I'd spend a week driving around Amboseli looking for cheetah, asking the game scouts where they'd seen them last, in an attempt to establish as accurate an estimate as possible of how many individuals were resident in the Amboseli area at that time. At the end of the week it seemed to me there were perhaps 8 to 10 females and 2 males and I couldn't see how, out of a population of 8 females, at least one of them wouldn't be pregnant. To cut a long story short I did find one, Violet Mary, and she was the animal who eventually featured in the programme.

The week I spent looking around and the subsequent search for a suitable female, were typically frustrating. There was simply no point in filming at that stage, even though I was running into situations every day which would have been well worth covering. What I was there for was to establish the existence, or otherwise, of a certain situation. Deliberately to turn a blind eye to everything else that was going on around me required a certain single-mindedness which didn't come all that easily.

Now, here I was going through it all over again, although this time the frustrations were of a somewhat different nature.

In general terms, the cheetah is in a fairly bad way in Eastern Africa. A lot of its former range has been taken over as farmland and where it does still exist it is a prime target for poachers. The plains of the eastern Serengeti, though, are one of the few areas left where cheetah appear to be flourishing. And what I had to decide was which part of the area I should choose to start working in. I doubted if I would get everything I wanted without moving around, but I had to start somewhere and since I had to pay National Park entrance fees, vehicle fees, camping fees and so forth, every day spent simply driving round looking for animals worth filming meant a larger hole was punched in my budget.

When I returned to Ndutu from my excursion to Dar-es-Salaam to send my exposed film to the UK for processing, Inky had some good news for me. To study her serval cats she had built a series of observation platforms erected in trees scattered through the woodland that fringes the top end of the Olduvai Gorge. From one of these she had seen on each of four successive days, a cheetah accompanied by two small cubs. What was more, the family wasn't too difficult to approach. If there was a 'tame' cheetah with cubs right on my doorstep, a good part of my problem had been solved on the very first day. So, after a day spent unpacking, getting myself organized again and generally settling in, we set out to find the female.

It was the dry season. The wildebeest had long since departed in the direction of Lake Victoria and now the plains were dusty and practically empty of large mammals. The animals that hadn't migrated were mostly concentrated around the few remaining sources of water. That meant there was a fairly heavy concentration of predators spread out around the shores of Lakes Lgarya and Marzak. We drove slowly around. Cheetah out hunting, or at any rate on the move, tend to move, at least in my experience, fairly erratically. They wander along for quite short distances and then, when a rise or a convenient patch of shade shows up, they flop down and lie there, quietly summing up the situation around them. Unless you are prepared to do much the same, your chances of seeing cheetah are considerably reduced. So what we were doing was driving slowly from one vantage point to another where I would have a good look round with the binoculars, sit for a while, perhaps have a cup of tea, anything to pass a little time, and then take another look around to see if the situation had changed. You have to give the game a chance to swing in your favour; to allow the cheetah an opportunity to get on its feet or put its head up. If you don't, you are very likely to see nothing at all in an area where, in fact, cheetah are really quite plentiful.

The first day out we spotted a rather wild cheetah that dived into some bushes at our approach. I couldn't see whether it was a male or a female. But on the off chance that it might have been the mother of the cubs, I sheered off, not wanting her to associate my Land Rover with an unpleasant experience and thus put her off me for good.

The day after that we saw 'The Brothers'. They were lying beside the track at the head of a long gulley. We stopped within feet of them and, as usual, they paid not the slightest attention to the car. People seeing two tame male cheetah together are apt to say 'We saw "The Brothers" today,' but in fact there are two such pairs living in that area. Both are tame, and by this I mean easily approachable, although whether they are in fact brothers is anyone's guess. Certainly this particular pair had almost identical markings on the backs of their ears, and this would be something of a coincidence if they weren't at least related. But no more concrete evidence than this exists to support the popular belief in their relationship. I refer to them in this way simply as a matter of convenience.

We paused for a few minutes to admire them and then moved on to continue looking for the female and her cubs. As a start, 3 cheetah in 2 days wasn't at all bad and I hadn't yet lost the air of what I can best describe as 'sceptical optimism' with which I approach the beginning of any new project. I never really believe things will go well. But since I don't actually have any proof that this will be the case I can't bring myself to be positively pessimistic. It wasn't long though before I changed my mind. A week later, having seen neither hide nor hair of a cheetah after those first two days, I was really beginning to feel a little gloomy.

People often say to me, on learning what I do for a living, 'Gosh, you must have a lot of patience,' or words to that effect. But it's only true up to a point. Of course I am patient. I seldom get bored sitting in a hide waiting for something to happen. But if this takes appreciably longer than estimated, I soon start wondering if I shouldn't be doing it some other way. After a week of driving round seeing nothing of what I was looking for, I decided the time had come to alter my tactics.

I thought back to my experiences with Violet Mary.

Violet Mary, as her pregnancy advanced, steadily grew heavier and heavier and for about the last fortnight was reduced to catching hares. Despite their speed, cheetah don't have all that much advantage over their prey. It is surprising how close they can come to an apparently unsuspecting target and still miss. It is as if the gazelle have a powerful spring coiled up inside them. The first hint of danger unlocks this and sets them running at top speed almost instantaneously. And if they can elude the cheetah for the first few hundred yards, they have a good chance of getting away with it entirely. The cheetah's endurance is strictly limited. This is why cheetah spend 99 per cent of their hunting time apparently sitting around doing nothing. In reality, of course, they are watching their potential prey for signs of weakness, for something that may increase their chances of success from a possibility to a probability. When you are watching cheetah, trying to understand what they are all about, you must never lose sight of the fact that, like all predators, the cheetah has to expend energy in order to secure its food. At the risk of repeating myself, it has to balance that expenditure against the likely return if it is successful. Consequently, it is not going to spend any more time than it can help, dashing around helter-skelter trying to grab healthy animals that have a better than average chance of escaping.

So, with every day that passed, Violet Mary grew heavier. And every day this fact progressively reduced the number of animals she could find against which she could still exert some leverage. Eventually, she reached the point at which about all she had a chance of catching was a one-eyed gazelle with three legs. And when we saw her turn her attention exclusively to catching hares we knew it couldn't be too long before she gave birth. The hare's only real form of defence seems to reside in its colouration and in the fact that if it stays perfectly still it is unlucky to be spotted. But this is only effective when the predator has its mind on other things. I have seen a pack of hunting dogs out after wildebeest trot right past a hare crouched in the grass. But against a hungry cheetah scanning the ground for a 'frozen' hare, this defence is doubly ineffective since the instinct to remain still until the predator is almost on top of it delivers it right into the cheetah's grasp.

Although Violet Mary's behaviour gave us a clear indication of what was about to happen, I was still taken by surprise when, early one morning, she disappeared into a papyrus swamp. It wasn't a place we could penetrate. And in any event, for the previous month, I had been doing my best not to get into a position from which, by coming round a bush too quickly or crashing through the undergrowth after her, I might have given her a nasty shock and made her nervous of me when she

Mixed herds on the Serengeti. Zebra often mingle with wildebeest during the migration.

A newborn wildebeest gets to its feet within minutes and starts to suckle almost immediately.

The moment of photographic truth. Vulture with slots open, flaps, landing gear and air brakes down.

Hunting dog puppies, outside the den, take exception to an Egyptian vulture.

eventually emerged with her cubs.

So we sat and looked at the green wall of the swamp confronting us and wondered. Had she really gone in there to have her cubs? The game scout I had with me was doubtful. He had never seen a cheetah at Amboseli use such a place. Had she simply gone in there because it was cool and damp against the heat of the day? Quite possible. Had she done it merely to get rid of us? I hoped not. All these thoughts passed through my mind as the minutes ticked away and Violet Mary failed to reappear. The game scout was all for driving round and round the swamp to look for places from which she might possibly emerge unseen from our present position. But if we did that and she came out at the same place where she had gone in, we would lose her. Either way there was a 50:50 chance of doing the wrong thing. That being the case, I decided to stay put and keep an eye on the spot at which I had last seen her. And in the end this paid off because just before sunset, having waited there throughout the day, I saw her head appear above the reeds momentarily and then sink down out of sight. Not much, but at least I knew she was still there.

Cheetah move around quite a lot on moonlit nights. But there was no moon, so I could be reasonably sure she would stay put in the swamp at least until dawn the next day. As the sun came up over the trees, there we were, muffled up against the cold wind streaming down off Kilimanjaro, watching for some sign of life from the swamp. Nothing. Time passed. The game scout became restless. He didn't mind sitting around doing nothing when he could see some sense in it. But now he wanted to move off and start searching. I was against this. The swamp was cool, it offered shade, and it also offered some protection against predators. Everything added up to the fact that Violet Mary was in there giving birth.

I resisted the pressure on me to move throughout that day, but by the evening I was having doubts as well. The following morning, when there was still no sign of Violet Mary, I gave in and we began to move around looking for signs that she might have passed. Slowly we widened the area of our search, visiting all her favourite resting places, spending hours at vantage points scanning the plains, but still nothing, not a sign of her. There was no alternative but to keep at it, for no other cheetah we knew of either had cubs or looked like having them. Unless I managed to re-locate Violet Mary I was right up the creek and no mistake. Already I had invested 6 weeks of time and energy into following her around. I was going to be decidedly unpopular if it all fell flat at the very time I had promised everyone it would pay off.

A week passed. No matter which way I looked at it Violet Mary had to be in that swamp. The alternative, that she had left the area altogether, was simply too appalling to contemplate. But while logic told me what the answer was the game scout felt otherwise. He had accompanied me on several occasions before. A member of the Wakamba, a hunting tribe, he had served in the King's African Rifles during the Second World War and had subsequently joined the Game Department. For over twenty years of his service he had been stationed at Amboseli and I had long since learned to disregard his advice at my peril. Now, his long years of experience in the area were leading him to a completely different answer from mine. Compared to him I was a complete novice. I also relied to a considerable extent on his goodwill. There were fairly strict regulations in force in the area at the time and if you stayed within the letter of the law it was just about impossible to achieve anything. So I relied heavily on his willingness to bend the rules when the occasion demanded it. Consequently I tended to go out of my way to humour him and pay attention to his views, even though I didn't necessarily agree with them.

There was one way, though, that I felt we could prove or disprove Violet Mary's presence, and that was to search along the edge of the swamp for her tracks. If she was still there, she had to have given birth by now. And if she had cubs she had to be feeding them. If she was feeding her cubs she had to be feeding herself. And to do that she had to come out and hunt. So, if she was entering and leaving the swamp, she had to be leaving tracks. My adviser wouldn't hear of it. She wasn't there, so it was a waste of time, and even if she was, there was too much grass for her tracks to show up. 'If you ask me,' said my wife, 'that's why he's against it. The old so and so's eyes are bad and he won't admit it.' I had to agree that this seemed a reasonable possibility. So, at the risk of provoking his displeasure, I went to the Warden with my problem and asked if I could borrow a tracker. One was produced and off into the swamp we went. Within minutes he came on cheetah tracks . . . and then more tracks . . . and more. They led in and out of the papyrus. Not only were there fresh ones, but old ones as well. There no longer seemed any doubt that Violet Mary had her cubs hidden in the swamp and that all the time we had been scouring the neighbourhood she had been slipping in and out of the papyrus unobserved. So next morning, we took up a suitable position and kept watch. Within half an hour Violet Mary appeared. Although I had been sure in my own mind that this would happen, when we actually saw her I can tell you I gave a big sigh of relief.

With that experience behind me, I decided that in my search on the Serengeti a change of tactics was called for. When a week of driving around Ndutu had failed to produce any worthwhile results, I called a halt. The expenditure of time and energy was getting me nowhere and I could no longer afford to have everything going out and nothing coming back in return. At this point, my mind went back to the tracker at Amboseli.

Every animal you work with comes better equipped to survive in its own environment than you do. It is invariably either stronger or faster or is possessed of more acute senses than a mere human being. All we have with which to redress the balance is our intelligence. If you don't make use of this, you aren't going to get very far. Some things you can't do much about. Your sense of hearing is one of them. But as far as cheetah are concerned that isn't much of an advantage. And smell? Well, I supposed it might be useful if you could detect them this way, but I doubt if it would be all that much of an advantage. Sight of course is the big factor. And here a decent pair of binoculars is a great help. But I suspected that at least part of my problem lay in the presence in the area of large numbers of lion. They too are affected by the lack of water on the plains during the dry season. There isn't much for them to eat out there either and so a population of lion which until recently had been distributed over a vast area of grassland had now concentrated in the woodland that fringed the Olduvai. I felt that this could be making the cheetah more than usually shy. On a previous occasion when I had spent some time filming 'The Brothers', they had departed in considerable haste at the appearance of a couple of lions so far away that I could barely make them out through binoculars. I had gone with them, and we had ended up a good 3 miles away with the pair invisible in the long grass growing up around a clump of bushes. You could have driven past a dozen times without getting even a hint of their presence. Clearly, something else in the way of a visual sense was called for.

The woodland is criss-crossed with a web of tracks along which its inhabitants go about their daily and nightly business. Upon them they leave, if not the clearest indications of their passing, at least signs that anyone who knew what he was looking for could interpret with a modicum of assurance. But the sad fact was that although I could make out the more obvious footpoints . . . lion, hyena and so forth . . . *provided* they had been placed on soil of the right consistency, the light was favourable, and no other animal had walked over them in the meantime, that simply wasn't enough. No, there was no doubt about it, what I needed was a tracker. But where to find one?

Alas, this was a problem that was going to have to wait for a solution. I could not afford to spend any more time on elusive cheetahs at this moment. Though they would play an important role in *Hunters*, they would only provide a small episode and I was fairly sure that I could get the hunts I needed at the end of my shooting schedule.

Lion kills would be something else however, and I needed a great deal of lion material which I knew would be hard to get on the plains: for some time I had been planning to move to the Ngorongoro Crater where lion were plentiful and more predictable. I had to stick to this plan and forget cheetah for the present.

8
A Film-maker's Diary

Television Specials are so costly to make that they only really make sense for both cameraman and producer if they carry some half-hours 'on their backs'. So one plans to film some half hour by-products in the same general area during the year or more that it takes to shoot material for the average one-hour Special. In the case of *Hunters*, we had evolved a most ambitious programme involving parallel half-hours on hunting dogs, cheetah and an area which I call the 'Eternal Triangle'. I'd better describe the 'Triangle' briefly.

The Triangle is an area close to Ndutu, just outside the Serengeti National Park into which the wildebeest migrate briefly. When they arrive there, the predators, the hunters of the plains, enjoy a brief heyday because there is temporarily plenty of food. Thus, the Triangle afforded me the material for its own half-hour as well as many splendid opportunities for filming predators for the Special.

By October, 1977, the Triangle and the plains nearby on which I had filmed the Genghis Pack had done everything they could do for me for the moment – except to provide filmable cheetah. I had all the dog footage I needed for both the Special and a dog half-hour. I also had one or two gems for *Hunters*. But if I wanted concentrated lion and hyena action for the Special, and I most certainly did, the Ngorongoro Crater was the best location. I shall describe this huge caldera, sometimes called the

'Eighth Wonder of the World', later. For the moment, though, I want to deal with the period surrounding the move. Moves in the field are always time-consuming. Time slips away appallingly fast during wildlife movie making. People who don't live our eccentric sort of life find it hard to imagine that we are ever put under pressure. Well, we most certainly are. We are under the pressure of deadlines just like anyone else in the film business, perhaps more so. Seasons and animal movements are like time and tide. They won't wait. Time just somehow trickles away.

So I thought that the best way I could show how this happens was to consult my diary for the month of October 1977, the period at which I had more or less made up my mind that the time had come to move from the plains around Ndutu to Ngorongoro, barely 50 miles away, in the Crater Highlands.

October 10
Yesterday I finally got the material I wanted to finish Eternal Triangle. The story involves the passing of the seasons and the effect this has on a small area of grassland on the eastern border of the Serengeti National Park. Early on in the proceedings I managed to film a golden jackal catching Thomson's gazelle. During the dry season, though, when the gazelle have left the plains the jackal no longer have this source of food available to them and they are reduced to searching for rodents and digging for beetles. I felt that if I could get film showing a jackal unearthing insects this would provide the editor with a good bridge between the wet and dry seasons. Getting what I wanted proved easier said than done though. Most golden jackal aren't at all keen on being followed by a vehicle but I eventually found a female who didn't seem to mind and settled into a routine which involved setting out from Ndutu in the early hours to reach her den just as it got light and she started off on her early morning hunt. I never saw her dig once though. She wandered along occasionally stopping to pick something up and chew it.

On a couple of occasions she scavenged from the carcass of a dead animal. As for digging, it simply didn't happen. Finally though, I had the camera running while she was sniffing around a bare patch of earth and a large lizard was incautious enough to emerge from its hole for a look around. Not very clever. The jackal had him in a flash and I was able to film her standing there with legs and tail dangling from her mouth. It wasn't exactly what I wanted but it would do. There was a time when I would have gone on doggedly trying to get her digging but nowadays filming costs just don't allow you this sort of luxury.

October 11
For some time now my Land Rover has been puffing out clouds of white smoke. No. 6 plug keeps oiling up. Oil is blowing out of the joint where the exhaust pipe joins the manifold. The mechanics at Ndutu shake their heads. One of their theories is that oil may be leaking past a valve seal and getting into the cylinder. But when I ask them to take the head off to take a look they refuse. Clearly they have considerable misgivings as to what they will find. Now that I'm making the move to Ngorongoro I can't afford the sort of delay that a serious breakdown would entail.

Jenny is due in from Nairobi in about 10 days and I have to go to Arusha to collect her. I decided to go early and deliver the car to the Land Rover agent in Arusha to get the trouble diagnosed and, hopefully, sorted out. It is a minor disaster. I would much prefer to use the time to prepare for the move to Ngorongoro. But it would be even more disastrous to damage the engine of the Land Rover.

October 12
Leave Ndutu later than anticipated but still in good time. However, I get even further behind schedule by calling in at the Ngorongoro Conservation office so decide to spend the night at Ngorongoro Safari Lodge instead of going on to Arusha.

A Film-maker's Diary

October 13
A message has come through to say that the Land Rover which has just been purchased by the Ngorongoro Safari Lodge has broken down at the Lake Manyara Hotel. So before going on to Arusha I drive to Manyara and tow it back. One does these favours all the time in Africa. With luck, or perhaps bad luck, you'll one day find yourself on the receiving end.

October 14
I go to the Land Rover agents in Arusha to ask them about the engine. They checked the compression and have found this okay on all cylinders. I ask them what they think of the car and they say it seems okay and short of taking the head off they can't do more. I ask them to do this but they refuse, saying they have no parts for a six cylinder. I tell them my wife is coming from Nairobi and could bring the spares with her. If they take the head off and find it needs a re-bore, crankshaft re-grind, new bearings, etc., what will this cost? The answer is so horrifying, I thank them kindly for their trouble and depart.

October 16
I spend the day in my hotel room trying to make some sense out of the accounts. On safari this isn't so easy. Most days I am out before first light and back after dark. By the time I've had a shower, eaten, cleaned the equipment and so forth, I've very little enthusiasm for book-keeping. So while Jenny is away, not much gets done so I've been hoping to use this week to get everything squared away before her return.

October 17
My inclination is to go and stand behind the authorities to make sure they get on with the work today, but I know this would be counter-productive and in any case I need to get a permit for my wife to cross the border at Namanga which is officially closed since the Kenya-Tanzania dispute. So I am at Police HQ by 7.30, which is the time they open in the morning. When Jenny

left for Nairobi, her exit permit stated that she would eventually return, so I take a copy of this along with me. The Regional Police Commander's secretary remembers the case and tells me there will be no difficulty about granting a permit for me to travel to the border to meet Jenny, but right now the RPC is out and I should come back tomorrow.

October 19
Back to Police HQ for my permit. Mrs Nasoro, the RPC's secretary, has gone to Dar. Her replacement knows nothing about the permit and sends me along the corridor to see another policeman. He listens to my story, phones the RPC's secretary and tells her I should see the RPC. I return from whence I came. There's one thing about being given the run-around in Tanzania. Everyone . . . well, almost everyone is so polite and cheerful it's difficult to get too annoyed. Even so I am slightly apprehensive by now since there is a rumour going round Arusha that the border is to be closed and that no one will be allowed in or out regardless. Someone is with the RPC and I must wait, but while I do I listen to an interesting conversation between a young Englishman who has been hitch-hiking in West Africa and one of those knowledgeable Americans who arrived in East Africa a couple of months ago and now seems to know everybody and everything. He tells the Englishman, who is heading for Nairobi, where to go for accommodation and who to contact, etc. etc., but before they get down to the real nitty-gritty, I am called into the RPC's office. He tells the girl that it's all right he has already approved the issue of the permit, gives her instructions as to how this should be made out and we leave. Outside, the two travellers have been joined by several more, all of whom are talking at the same time recounting their experiences in several different countries and while the girl is setting up the paper in her typewriter, several turn their attention to her with requests for this, that and the other. A policeman arrives with a load of paperwork, the telephone rings. The

girl is beginning to get upset. After all she is only a temporary stand-in and doesn't really know what she is doing. What she should really do is kick the bloody lot out (except for me, of course) and deal with one thing at a time. She simply doesn't know what on earth to write on the paper so I leave, assuring her that I will return first thing next day. I am not keen on this because Jenny is arriving tomorrow but I am not going to get anywhere right now and under the circumstances it seems the most useful contribution I can make.

October 20
I can hardly believe it. We set out from Arusha with all vehicles serviceable and the right number of permits on board, heading for the border at Namanga. My stars must have been favourable. There are two police barriers to pass through on the way but usually we have no difficulty at either and the only problem en route is one puncture on the Land Rover. After a short wait at the Customs post I see Jenny arrive at Kenya Customs. A friend of ours in Nairobi, Ali Mawani, an old aquaintance of mine from my flying days, has lent her a truck in which to transport our belongings.

When Tanzania and Kenya both belonged to the East African Community they shared a common Customs Service. Now that the Community has split up it won't be long before each country has its own Customs, but this hasn't happened yet. The Customs officials of both countries still serve within the same organization. Consequently, Jenny has been able to have all our togs and chattels inspected by Customs in Nairobi, sealed by them and certified as 'personal possessions'. This is important. Entering Tanzania for the first time you are allowed to bring 'personal possessions' duty and sales-tax free. So she is allowed through both Customs posts without having her cases examined. Instead, she has to report to Customs in Arusha with the seals unbroken. There the contents are checked and, all being well, we will then be able to take them away.

Hunters of the Plains

At the second police barrier though we run into trouble. The police want us to open the crates. I explain that this will mean breaking the seals, which we are not allowed to do. But if the police wish to do so of course that's up to them, but in that case they must stamp the Customs form to certify that they have done so. I hope to heaven they don't as we'll be in Arusha for evermore sorting that one out, but of course I can't say anything else. The police are suspicious. Clearly they smell some form of jiggery-pokery in progress. We both advance our respective arguments several times. Finally the commander of the detachment arrives. The situation is explained once again. He delivers his verdict. We must travel to Arusha under police escort, leave everything at the police station overnight, bring a Customs official next morning and open everything then. 'Is that alright?' 'Of course,' we say. 'Whatever you say.' Unfortunately, no one is keen to come with us to Arusha, and while they are still discussing who should go, a man pushes his way through the throng surrounding the drama, for we have been there an hour by now, and there is a considerable queue of cars on either side of the barrier. The newcomer proclaims himself a Customs officer on his way to Namanga. The police explain that they want to look inside the crates, but don't want to break the seals so they are sending someone to Arusha with us. 'No need,' says the Customs man. 'Those seals are a guarantee that what is in those boxes is what it says on those lists. A guarantee,' he repeats. Immediately the situation is transformed. Everyone smiles. We shake hands with all concerned. 'Sorry for the delay,' they exclaim, 'but we have to guard the interests of our country.' We climb back into the cars and depart before they change their minds.

October 21
We go to a clearing agent and have a 'Nil Sales Tax' entry prepared and then head for the Customs, hoping that we will be able to leave for Ndutu the next day since driving on Sundays is

prohibited after 2 p.m. to save petrol and if we don't get away soon we will be stuck in Arusha for the weekend. Adrian and Sally Moyes have taken pity on us and we are now staying with them in Arusha and I hate to lumber them with us any longer than is necessary. However, the accountant who is the only person who can approve the 'Nil Entry' is away on safari, and so nothing can be done to release our belongings and we are advised to go away and return the next day.

October 22
While I rush around town doing some last minute shopping, Jenny goes back to Customs. Eventually she returns triumphant. Everything is now is order. We can take our things and go. It is 11 o'clock.

October 23
We set out for Ndutu more or less as planned with Jenny driving the Range Rover and me with the Land Rover. We plan to stay the night at the Ngorongoro Safari Lodge. It's such a restful, attractive place it's no hardship at all.

Going up the escarpment after Manyara the throttle linkage on the Land Rover breaks. To repair it is a simple job, but the only way to get your hand far enough into the engine compartment is to tie the bonnet up onto the windscreen and stand on the cylinder head. The engine is so hot though that it's going to take an age to cool down. So we hitch the Range Rover onto the Land Rover and pull both it and the trailer, all three vehicles loaded to the gills, to the lodge where we have tea and let things cool down before sorting the trouble out. The Range Rover is tremendously impressive when it comes to this sort of thing.

October 24
Flat tyres this morning that had to be repaired before we could start, but otherwise no problems on the journey and we got into Ndutu in one piece in mid-afternoon.

October 25
A note from a scientist, George Frame at Seronera. The Serengeti Research Institute is carrying out a predator census on 28/29 October. They are short of vehicles. Could I bring my Land Rover? George has been so helpful in the past there is no way I can, or would want to, refuse. We spend these two days unpacking and then re-packing ready for our move from Ndutu to Ngorongoro Crater where I am to start filming lion and hyena.

October 27
At Seronera we are given a map with the transects we are required to cover and the arrangements made to get to our startline the next morning. On arrival at George's house he said: 'Didn't you get my message? I sent to tell you that we have two cheetah with small cubs only a few kilometres away. We've been expecting you all week.' The message never reached me. So now what do we do? I hate to change plans. It seldom pays. But I have a half-hour to film on cheetah and material on young cubs is something I really need.

October 28
Up at 4.45 in order to get to our start point at the right time. Everyone gathers at George's for a quick coffee first and then we are off. The actual driving of the transects is uneventful. It takes us through country with which I had become pretty familiar while filming wild dogs earlier in the year so I think we stayed on track pretty well. A lot of the time spent discussing the whys and wherefores of the cheetah situation though. I finally decide that we really ought to postpone our move to Ngorongoro for a short while as the potential return from the cheetah is too great to miss.

After we had finished our count and were returning to Seronera, Rebecca noticed some lion sitting under a tree – 3 adult females and 8 cubs of varying size. So we drove over to look at them. Within 5 minutes one female got up and stalked a small family of wart-hogs. Moving stealthily off along a line of bushes she kept glancing back at the group under the tree. Then another lioness moved off in the opposite direction, the two of them converging on the wart-hog from either side. Finally, the third female crept up on them mid-way between the others. Suddenly the wart-hogs panicked and ran. One of them broke in the wrong direction and was immediately seized by two lionesses. It didn't go far amongst two hungry lions but everyone appeared to get something. Submerged beneath the mass of lion there was little wart-hog to be seen. Rebecca watched with interest. But when a few odds and ends of wart-hog plumbing began to appear from the depths she said 'I think I should like to go now.'

Interesting, but irritating since this is exactly what I am going to Ngorongoro to try and film and in view of the fact that we were supposed to be counting animals I had left the camera behind!!!

October 29
Day two of the count. Our transects today took us almost back to Ndutu so instead of returning to Seronera we gave our results to James Malcolm, the lion expert, who took them back for us.

October 30
Having sorted all our gear out for the Ngorongoro trip we now re-sort it to accommodate the entirely different conditions at Seronera. I am uneasy. Logic tells me that I should go to Seronera. There are two families of cheetah there and families of cheetah are what I need. Something else though, experience I suppose you could call it, is telling me the opposite.

October 31
We drive to Seronera only to find when we get there that the cheetah with the five cubs has lost her entire family. It appears that she is still looking for them. It seems as if my premonition was correct.

Hunters of the Plains

November 1
We spend the day at Seronera on a recce and see two things. One cub of the remaining family climbs onto a branch for a few seconds and then descends into the thicket in which its mother is hiding. The cheetah that has lost her cubs walks slowly off along the skyline on her own. Jenny and I look at each other. The situation has 'waste of time' stamped all over it, I'm afraid. We say our farewells to George. It was very kind of him to have passed on the information but it simply isn't going to work.

November 2
We leave for Ndutu and are fortunate enough to see the Genghis Pack en route, the group of Cape hunting dogs I filmed for *Hunters* earlier on. They had a litter of thirteen pups in March and two of them still survive. One of the young females has broken a leg though and it seems impossible that she can keep up with them much longer. I'm afraid she is doomed.

November 3
We spend the day re-packing for Ngorongoro.

November 4
About 15 miles from Ndutu I get out to check the trailer and discover the rear right-hand spring has parted company with the rest of the car. By an incredible stroke of luck it is now sitting firmly on its attachment bracket so I return to Ndutu very gingerly and manage to get back without disturbing it. The garage sets to work to fix it although this takes all day. We will try again tomorrow.

November 5
We get away at 6.30 a.m. and reach Ngorongoro without incident. There we collect a new African driver called Martin as my old driver decided to leave me in Arusha. We are also obliged to pick up a game guard called Simon. Simon belongs to the Ngorongoro Conservation Authority who administers the Crater. The background to this is as follows. Apparently a bunch of

Maasai moran – warriors who in this case have turned out to be, uncharacteristically, a group of tearaways – have been robbing tourist camps. So the Authority has 'suggested' that we have a game guard along while we are working in the Crater. Normally, this is a thing I'm not very keen on. These guys, however pleasant and well-meaning, are usually just in the way, sitting around camp, leaning on dusty and ancient ·303 rifles and picking their noses. One has the feeling that they probably won't know how to use the rifle if ever the need arises. But there are other aspects to this. First, it's just as well to fall in with the Authority's requirements. For a start, they've been extremely helpful to me. Second, there's no harm in having someone around camp to keep an eye on the place when we are out filming. These lads are quite often co-operative, helping to chop wood and so on. I expect while we're in the Crater we'll get to know a whole succession of them. The Authority changes them around every two weeks or so. So we welcome young Simon aboard. Rebecca is very impressed with Simon as he carries a gun. We drive to the bottom of the Crater and put up our tents.

November 6
Martin and I return to Ndutu in the Range Rover to collect the camera equipment which I had left behind there to lighten the load. On the way back we are picking our way slowly over one especially bad patch of rocks when a Land Rover passes us doing about 50 miles an hour. I swear if I had had my elbow out of the window he would have had my arm off. He disappears up Ngorongoro going like a rocket and later on we pass tracks which show where he left the road in a muddy patch and careered along in the ditch for twenty or thirty yards. It still makes me go cold to think of what might have happened.

November 7
This is the first day since 10 October that I have done any serious filming. It's unbelievable. All that time gone and yet I

can't see how any of it was avoidable. There is just one consolation though. This morning we found a 'tame' cheetah that I would bet you anything is pregnant. She is an enormous size. She looks uncomfortable when lying down. She frequently licks her belly as if something is irritating her. Her rear legs have an odd twitch as if something might be pressing on a nerve somewhere. Once she leapt to her feet as if a spring had been released inside her. Was she feeling cubs moving inside her?

We stay with her until dusk falls. Cheetah don't move around much at night unless there's a moon and I would like to follow her again tomorrow. As we drive back to camp I find my spirits have risen sharply. Throughout this last month I have been getting more and more frustrated. I seem to be caught in some dreadful quagmire. I struggle hard to make progress but only get deeper into the mire. If someone had offered me a half-decent job in an office I'd have taken it like a shot. But now that we've seen cheetah I'm on top of the world. Wouldn't change my job for anything!!

November 8
Although we are back at the Munge river where we saw the cheetah yesterday, shortly after first light she is nowhere to be seen. We climb to the top of a nearby hill and search the Crater floor with binoculars. Then we descend and drive slowly along both banks of the Munge. Not a hint of cheetah. Finally, we go to a small hill. This is a flat-topped structure called Enkitati by the Maasai because in Maasai, the word means 'belt' and there is a belt of rocks along its slopes. From the top we look carefully along the length of the Mandusi swamp. My guess is that this is where the cheetah will go to have her cubs. She will hide them in the reeds in a damp part where it will be difficult for other predators to penetrate. On the other hand Martin, who has been a guide in Ngorongoro for 10 years and tells me he has never seen a cheetah with small cubs in the Crater in all that time, clearly feels that she will go high up on to the wall and give

birth in the cover up there where we have little chance of discovering her hideaway. He could well be right, but I daren't believe it.

After the morning's search we returned to camp to collect all our available fuel containers and drive to Ngorongoro village for petrol. Just as we are leaving, the people in the next camp site drive up. Their camp has just been raided and they could see a Maasai making off into the distance with assorted items of camp gear, clothing etc. So maybe we do need a game guard. They wanted to borrow Simon. I was rather sceptical when Mr Mgina the Conservator had insisted that we have a game scout to guard the camp against intruders. So Simon sets off with the visitors. The Maasai throws rocks at them as they approach him and hits Simon twice. Simon fires over his head as a warning. The rifle does work after all. The Maasai is captured and they take him to the police post. He will get anything between 5 and 15 years and there is no chance he will get off as he has been inside for this sort of thing before.

November 9
No sign of cheetah today, but plenty of lion around. I do a little filming, mainly of a newly-born Thomson's gazelle staggering to its feet, being cleaned by its mother, feeding from her and so on. But it is good to be out in clear weather with nothing else to do except film. The car is running well. We have fuel and food and film and, for the time being, I have nothing else to do except what I am here for and that is to sit behind the camera. Would you believe it? A month has gone by. During the course of it I haven't once had a day off, and I've managed only 4 days serious filming. If this was a typical month, of course, we'd be out of business. But it would be typical if you didn't watch out. People are hospitable: they ask you out and you can't always refuse. People are interested in what I do and they want to talk, and even if you are itching to get away and start cleaning equipment or something of the sort, you can't do it or you are thought to be

rude. Everything takes longer, and every day you spend chasing spare parts or waiting for repairs or for the Customs man to turn up, it costs you money to live and you aren't earning anything to offset the drain. So it's worrying and sooner or later you have to shut it all out and go to work and to hell with everyone because the people whose money you are spending aren't interested in excuses. No one wants to know why you didn't succeed.

9
The Hyena

'The Eighth Wonder of the World' is a fair description of the Ngorongoro Crater, although, of course, it doesn't quite fit in with the other seven wonders since it is of natural origin.

Crater is rather a misnomer. The strictly accurate term is caldera, which means a collapsed volcanic crater worn away by erosion and reduced in size by earth movements and other unimaginable forces. There have been plenty of those over the past 20 million years in the Crater Highlands of Tanzania.

What the Ngorongoro caldera can have been like when it really was a crater, or rather an active volcano, I cannot begin to picture. Today it resembles a gigantic soup plate. The existing walls are some 2,000 feet high. Wall to wall it is between 10 and 12 miles wide. Its floor covers an area of 102 square miles. Someone worked out that you could deposit most of Paris and its suburbs inside the caldera, and this I can well believe.

Much of the floor consists of short grass plains, ideal for grazing animals, though there is a surprising wealth of different habitats, albeit in miniature. There is a soda lake used by water birds and sometimes by flamingo; a stream called the Munge, swamps, minor hills, including one named Enkitati, and a small forest, the Lerai, in which the Tanzanian Authorities once proposed to build a tourist hotel but were fortunately stopped by weight of conservation opinion. Instead, they far more sensibly built two new lodges on the Crater rim and made roads far more negotiable than the original hair-raising track which existed back in the 1960s from the then one primitive but really rather delightful lodge.

Having the lodges on the rim means that tourists can only visit the Crater floor by day and must be back at their base by nightfall. Living in the Crater was a privilege afforded by the Ngorongoro Conservation Authority to Jenny, Rebecca and myself when we were filming, and, of course, to various research scientists.

The only other human inhabitants of Ngorongoro are a few hundred Maasai who have two *manyattas*, or villages, there. The Crater lies in the heart of Maasailand and the integration of these pastoral warrior nomads with the environment and the wildlife is part of the Conservation Authority's basic policy. Maasai are peaceful people, though, as I have said, there had been trouble with a bunch of moran, young warriors, who had been robbing tourists' camps. It was for this reason that the Authority requested that we attached a game guard to our strength, as I have already recounted. So I was resigned to having a succession of these during our stay.

As far as *Hunters* was concerned Ngorongoro was ideal because it has an unbelievably rich resident population of plains animals – eland, zebra, wildebeest, gazelle, even rhino, and of course lion and hyena.

To be more precise it contains at least 300 hyenas and around 100 lions. I had come to the Crater to film these lions and hyenas hunting and to record the defensive mechanisms of the animals they were trying to catch. Easily said, but how would I go about this, given that both lion and hyena tend to hunt more at night than in daylight?

First I had to try and understand how the predators themselves are organized. One thing is certain: they aren't just walking around down there in a purely haphazard manner. If nothing else, they need to keep fairly close to their food supply. Then again, they have a social structure within which they are compelled to operate and this, in its turn, imposes certain restraints on their movements.

As for the lion population of the Crater, I was lucky. Two scientists, Doctors David and Jeanette Bygott, had been studying the Ngorongoro lion for over 2 years. The Bygotts generously gave me a map showing which prides were currently occupying which areas and a set of notes to indicate how I might recognize the various groups when I came across them. Not all research workers are so helpful. Photographers have been known in the past to accept information of this kind and subsequently pass it off as their own work. Consequently, there is often an understandable reluctance on the part of the scientific community to part with their hard-won knowledge. The Bygotts' kindness got me off to a flying start.

The only information I had on the Crater's hyena came from Hans Kruuk's study which he completed in 1968 and which was therefore, at least as far as territorial boundaries were concerned, hardly up to date. One of the most interesting and visible aspects of hyena behaviour in Ngorongoro is the strict determination between the ground occupied by adjacent clans. Hans Kruuk, who worked at the Serengeti Research Institute, was able to work out where these boundaries lie by means of an extensive marking programme. He first immobilized 51 hyenas with a dart gun and then cut notches in their ears so that the individuals became easily recognizable even at a fair distance. Later, by noting which hyenas he saw, and where, he was able to work out where these boundaries between the clans, as he called them, occurred. This sort of thing is acceptable in the name of science, but any photographer who asked for permission to go round marking the hyena population of Ngorongoro in this way would create an impression of himself that it would take several light years to dispel. So in order to make sense out of the current situation I had to work another way.

Hyena, unlike lion, tend (at least in the Crater) to keep their young in certain well established communal dens. The location of most of these are quite well known and the first thing I did was to get Martin to drive me around to all the major sites so that I could mark them on my map and at the same time assess their potential from a photographic standpoint. Having done this, I decided that I would confine my attention to three clans only because to try to cover the whole lot was clearly impossible. The three selected appeared, on the face of it, to offer the best possibilities.

Next, I did my best to take still pictures, left, right and full frontal, of each hyena I saw lying around the dens. Since no hyena from another clan would be permitted to come so close to the young, there could be no possible doubt as to which clan these animals belonged. Not far off, other hyena would be lying. Some of these were young that had left the nursery and taken up residence in some desirable accommodation close at hand, but still returned to the den each evening to play. Others were adults, of course. Some of these were more welcome at the den than others. You could be sure that all these were members of the same clan, simply because they were accepted in the general area of the den.

The allegiances of hyena seen further from the den were more doubtful. If two hyena dens are, let us say, 6 kilometres apart, you cannot assume that the clan boundary lies half-way between. So I set about photographing groups of hyena as well. Sometimes we would come across a number feeding amicably together, or lying around in a muddy patch. You could be sure that all these came from the same clan. But which one? I kept pictures obtained in this way in sets. So if I saw one of these individuals show up at a den or noticed it socializing with a hyena whose loyalties were known, I could then label the entire group. In this way I gradually built up my knowledge of the local population. By keeping a close check on where I saw them all, I began to have some idea of the clan structure generally.

It was a slow business. Getting the still pictures was one thing. Using them was another thing altogether. Some of the individuals were easily recognized, even at a distance. Often, however, they were caked in mud which completely obscured their spot patterns. I began to realize how useful it would have been to identify individuals by their ears alone. However, from a film-making point of view, the effort was well worth it. Before long I had a fair idea where the boundaries lay between at least three clans and accordingly where I was most likely to see groups of hyena scent-marking their frontiers. Thus, I knew in advance those areas where conflicts were most likely to occur.

When I started writing this book I determined that it would not be about animal behaviour, but about filming animals. In the first place I'm not a behaviourist. I have come to realize that the more I see of animals the less I know about them. On the other hand, filming them is something I do know about. There have been a number of books published in recent years that detail, almost on a minute to minute basis, the actions of a particular animal or group of animals. While I admired the success of such books, I cannot say I really enjoyed them. I soon got fed up with reading about how George got up and licked Fred, walked over and scratched a tree and so forth. I was determined not to drift into something of the kind myself. I have to admit, though, that once you begin to recognize individuals, their relationships with each other and all the behaviourist detail they go through to maintain such relationships, it does make life, as a photographer, more interesting. Driving from A to B you learn to watch out for certain characters who favour certain areas and wonder where they are if you don't see them. When sitting at a den, for instance, your ability to predict what is likely to happen upon the approach of, let us say, Henry or Henrietta, can't help but enhance your work. But as a photographer you must resist becoming too fascinated by the minutiae on which the scientists are hooked.

Identifying predators and predicting their actions is difficult enough. Catching those actions on film is even harder. There are, as you might expect, several schools of thought on how to go about it. Just like the predator, the cameraman has to balance the cost of his actions against the possible return from them. In theory, given enough money, almost anything is possible. But this seldom happens in real life. You constantly have to try and stretch whatever resources are available to you in such a way as to close the inevitable gap between what you need and what you've actually got in the kitty.

Sitting still in one place is, of course, by far the most economic system to adopt both in terms of fuel and wear and tear on the vehicle. But it is highly uneconomic in terms of man-hours unless you guess right most of the time about where the action is most likely to occur.

The Scratching Rocks, after which one hyena clan was named, protruded from a small hillock that rose from the north-eastern part of the central plains. In Hans Kruuk's day the rocks lay on the boundary between the two clans. I don't know why he called them 'the Scratching Rocks'; but one of the ways in which hyenas mark out their boundaries is by scratching up the earth with their feet. And if the Scratching Rocks lay on a recognized boundary then there would almost certainly have been a lot of scratching going on there so I suppose that's how the place got its name.

I was very soon to witness the boundary system in action. One morning, shortly after six, we came upon a small group of hyena chasing a herd of wildebeest. They weren't being all that enthusiastic about it but even so they gave me some nice film. The significant thing about the incident was the fact that their activity attracted the attention of twelve other hyena who came running up from the direction of the Scratching Rocks, their tails held high, a clear indication that they were excited about something. Their approach brought seven more hyena running to the scene, but this time from a completely different direction, from 'The Castle', the communal den of the Lakeside clan.

When the original hunters spotted these two parties bearing

down on them they soon lost interest in what they were doing and pushed off through the swamp in the general direction of the small hill called Enkitati. The wildebeest didn't hang around either and that left the twelve Scratching Rocks and the seven Lakeside hyena facing each other. They shuttled back and forth. First one group advanced and then the other. But it was noticeable that there was no physical contact on either side. The Lakesiders would advance and the Scratching Rocks group retreat ahead of them. But when the Lakesiders reached what was a clearly recognizable boundary as far as they were concerned, they abruptly turned and retreated. At this it was the Scratching Rocks hyenas' turn to advance. And so it went on until honour was apparently satisfied all round. They broke off the engagement and, with a final burst of scratching, wandered off into the security of their respective territories.

Clearly, here was one point that could be plotted on the boundary map. For film-making it was a valuable piece of information for it meant that we could return to the same spot and be reasonably certain that parties of hyena would come by at intervals and scent-mark, a process I needed to film sooner or later. It also gave me forewarning that any lion kills in that general area would almost certainly result in some interesting hyena material as well.

Two days later we were able to extend the point into a line. Passing the same part of the swamp we spotted a Scratching Rocks group out scent-marking. Since we hadn't located any lion at that time we decided to break off our search and follow the marking party for a while. There were thirteen of them. They marched steadily along and at certain evidently familiar landmarks they would settle down for a good scratch, to defecate (another marking method much used by hyena), and to 'paste'. Pasting is a system which involves drawing a stem of grass between their hind legs and in this way depositing a glandular secretion which can be recognized by other hyena. When hyena meet, a tremendous amount of sniffing goes on and I don't doubt that this has something to do with the need to recognize the scent of a considerable number of other hyena as and when the occasion demands.

As the marking party advanced towards the marsh where we had seen the previous encounter take place, I noticed, just ahead of it, a pair of ears sticking up out of the grass. I didn't place any particular significance on this event at that moment. All it meant to me was that there was a hyena resting at that spot. Hyena rested in the grass everywhere. The present estimate of the Ngorongoro population is between 300 and 600 individuals so one more pair of ears doesn't mean too much – under normal circumstances. But this time, the circumstances weren't normal. The ears belonged to an unfortunate character who had chosen to doze just, as it were, on the wrong side of the fence.

At least I assume that's what he was doing because the Scratching Rocks party were all around him before he realized what was going on and rose to his feet. He stood there, tail between his legs in a submissive attitude while they checked on his identity. When they had made up their minds about him, one Scratching Rocks hyena seized him by the side of the neck while another grabbed hold of his left hind leg and began to twist. A few simply stood around and watched, but most of them quite slowly and deliberately began to take him apart. I could see his head raised above the backs of the aggressors, his teeth bared in an enforced grin. He began to utter a series of howls and chattering shrieks as more and more teeth sank into his flanks.

For a while I thought they were actually going to kill him, but they eventually let him go and he stood there looking rather dazed as one by one they lost interest and meandered off into Scratching Rocks land to return to their chosen resting places for the remainder of the day. Their victim hobbled off through the swamp towards Enkitati, and I began to wonder if in fact this wasn't a point on the Scratching Rocks boundary that

Yearling wildebeest caught at both ends by the dogs. Chances of escape now are almost nil.

Despite the occasional tussle over food, hunting dogs live a peaceful, organised life as a pack.

'I filmed an unusual sequence of jackals, normally lowly scavengers, hunting young Thomson's gazelle.'

John Pearson with his daughter Rebecca, who, with Jenny his wife, shared many safaris with him, including his last one.

The Hyena

adjoined two neighbouring clans. The hyena we had seen hunting there before had gone off into the swamp. And now today's encounter had failed to provoke any response from the Lakeside clan, several of whom were lying within sight of the struggle and I'd have thought would have been tempted to join in. It was a point worth bearing in mind.

Hyena, like most predators, are potentially dangerous even to their own kind. But naturally, there have to be limits to this. This is one of the advantages of being territorial. Hyena young born within a certain territory, live within a communal den to which the male members of the community have restricted access, for they will certainly eat them if they get the opportunity. Certain males are tolerated either at or close to the den, but most of them know better than to venture near since the females are pretty formidable characters.

Gradually the cubs learn to recognize other individuals, both in their own age group and amongst the adults. They also learn the complex sign language by means of which hyena order their existence. As the Scratching Rocks party ambled slowly back into their territory, the closer they came to the communal den the more young hyena they encountered. These were cubs old enough to leave the immediate vicinity of the den and lie by themselves during the daytime. In the evening they would return to the den to play there and to meet their mothers, but for the rest of the time they were on their own. On the approach of the marking party, each juvenile rose to his feet and faced the oncoming group with what appeared to be apprehension. Without exception, each allowed the adults to approach within a few feet and then bolted. In the light of the incident we had just witnessed, this was obviously a wise precaution. As a hyena, if you aren't absolutely certain who is approaching you, or of your ability to establish your own identity, it is clearly sensible not to take any chances.

These are the sort of insights into the behaviour of the animals you are filming that are essential for a cameraman.

Hunters of the Plains

Once you are able to anticipate what is likely to happen, you stand at least half a chance of getting just that little bit ahead of the action that may make all the difference between ordinary and outstanding material. Even so, you still have to be circumspect. Like some wines, these sort of situations, 'tasted' on their own home ground, are often unforgettable. But all too frequently they don't travel too well. You have to try and visualize what reaction your material will provoke when viewed in London. You get to know the individual animals concerned, and how they are likely to react under certain circumstances. Accordingly, when you see film of them afterwards you invest it with your private knowledge and this is almost impossible to impart to anyone else. Television isn't a particularly subtle medium as far as wildlife filming is concerned. So however frustrating it may be at times, the cameraman is well advised to keep it simple and straightforward. Don't waste time trying to capture too many 'small' actions. It's unlikely to enhance your reputation for anything except 'over-shooting'.

The hyena is such a formidable animal when operating within the context of its own society that it isn't difficult to invest it with a kind of invincibility that it doesn't actually possess. It is in its relationship with lion that you see it brought down to size most effectively. Most of the practical knowledge I was beginning to acquire on the subject of hyena was actually being accumulated while following lion. It was while hurrying off one morning in search of one of the prides that I later came to know as the 'Tokitok Ten' that we ran into a situation that gave me yet another insight into the nature of hyena.

We were just about to turn off the Enkitati track, bound for the east side of the Madusi swamp, when, ahead of us, I noticed a vehicle. It was David and Jeanette's Land Rover. I took a closer look at them through the binoculars in case they might have broken down and needed some help. As I lifted the glasses a burst of roaring broke out just ahead and across the plains towards us ran a lioness and two well-grown female cubs being seen off the premises in no uncertain fashion by one of the Munge Pride males. Behind him I could make out more males and a host of silver-backed jackal. One of the Munge males was feeding off the remains of a wildebeest.

I waited until the sun came up and then filmed him eating one end of the carcass while jackals ate from the other. Nearby, several females sat around waiting to get at the meat when his lordship had finished.

After we had been there about 10 minutes hyena calls not far off indicated that something else was happening. Perhaps three-quarters of a mile further on we found another of the Munge males eating from yet another wildebeest carcass. David and Jeanette told me afterwards that hyena from the Seneto clan had killed both wildebeest just before dawn but had been chased off their kills by the Munges, of which there were no fewer than five (males) present in all.

I filmed the scrum of jackal and hyena that descended on the remains when the lion left and then followed this lion back towards the other kill. As we approached I could see that there was still an argument going on around the remains. But from the attitude of the male closest to us, it looked rather as if he had actually caught something on his own. We changed direction and went over to him. At first I thought he had a wart-hog, but when we drew closer I could see that the lion had in fact got hold of a hyena. He had his teeth sunk into its neck and his paws were clasped about the forepart of its body. At intervals a deep rumbling came from the lion. It shook its head and tightened its grip as if the hyena was still struggling. I couldn't see any sign of this myself but clearly the lion was responding to some movement on the part of the hyena so my guess is that a purely involuntary spasm was wracking the hyena's body from time to time. It was this that was annoying the lion.

Finally, the lion got to it's feet and half-dragged, half-carried the hyena off the mud flat on which it had been resting and dropped it onto the grass. Not surprisingly, it lay there motionless. At this, another of the Munge males who had been sitting nearby and not, apparently, taking any special interest in the proceedings, walked slowly across and stood gazing down at the hyena. I looked at the trio through my glasses. To my amazement I could see that the hyena was still breathing. Whether it then opened an eye or twitched a muscle or whether the second male was simply showing his dislike for hyena in general, I have no idea. Whatever the reason, the lion literally slammed down onto it, sank its teeth into its back and shook and twisted it in a quite appalling display of ferocity.

Twice the lion left. Twice one of them returned, picked up the hyena and drove its teeth deep into its flesh. And still it lived. In fact, on the last occasion both Martin and I thought the hyena actually turned and snapped at the lion although it hardly seemed possible that it could have any fight left in it at this stage. Finally, after the lion had gone, two other hyena came up and examined it closely, sniffing its body and paying great attention to the ground nearby which must have fairly reeked of lion. At about 9.15, just as the second of the two visitors was wandering off, a groan came from the wounded animal. The departing hyena stopped and looked back. I picked up my binoculars. There was no longer any sign of life.

For a while I watched to see what would happen. Various hyena stopped to examine the corpse. One licked it briefly. Another took hold of one flank and pulled the dead animal over onto its other side. But I saw no sign of any inclination to eat it – and hyena will eat most things. Eventually, we went up to take a closer look at the corpse. It was difficult to make out the extent of the damage to the hyena's throat as its fur concealed most of this, but it was easy to believe that the lion's canines must have met somewhere inside. Its back, where the second male had gripped it, looked far worse.

The whole episode left me with a very uncomfortable feeling. Not, I think, because of the awe-inspiring display of strength we had just witnessed. You frequently see examples of that

The Hyena

around a kill. It was the manner in which it was applied that made me shudder. The first male might conceivably have had some reason for savaging the hyena. But as far as the second was concerned it is difficult for the human mind to grasp what it was that brought about the sudden outburst. If the lion had been enraged you might have expected it at least to hasten towards its victim. But no! It sauntered slowly across, stood looking down for a few seconds and then the transformation to sheer, apparently unmotivated savage rage occurred.

I had seen a lot of ferocity in pursuit of *Hunters of the Plains* but this for some reason really shook me.

10
The Lion

I was under no illusions about what would prove the most difficult part of the filming. It was no mistake that my original proposal for *Hunters* didn't include lion or hyena. I chose hunting dogs and cheetah for a number of reasons, mainly because they were daytime hunters, but also because once you have located the right dog/cheetah situation, everything else falls into line. Even the hyena problem was really only one of timing. It was lion that had me worried.

With dogs, what you look for is a pack with pups in a den. Once you have found that you can drive there every day and know you will see something happen. With cheetah, you look for a female about to have cubs and then, provided you can locate her hiding place, all you have to do is wait outside until she emerges and follow her, knowing full well that she has only come out for one thing – to kill.

With hyena, too, you have a datum point from which to work – the communal nursery. It may not be where the hunts start from, but you know that the clan are lying all round it and this limits the area you have to search in order to find the action.

It doesn't work that way with lion. They may be anywhere within their territory, which can extend over as much as 100 square miles. Finding them, let alone filming them hunting, represents a real headache. It was for this reason that I chose the Ngorongoro Crater when the time came to start filming them.

At least within its bounds I knew that there were at least 60 or 70 resident lion. A lot was known about the hunting areas used by the various prides, and, if this didn't tell you exactly where they were, at least it narrowed the search area very considerably.

As the days went by we came to recognize more and more of the Ngorongoro lion. David and Jeanette Bygott had very kindly explained their identification system to me and we stopped alongside as many lion groups as we could, counted spots, made diagrams of ears and all the rest of it. At first it was necessary to do this with virtually every lion. But then I began to realize that I was sketching individuals I had seen before and I would look back in my notebook and sure enough there she was '09.15 near Munge River. Badly scarred right ear. Only three incisors.' Hardly what you'd call a friend but at least an acquaintance.

At this stage it becomes tiresome not to have names for individuals. Otherwise you get involved in long conversations trying to decide whether the two of you are really talking about the same animal.

Me: You see that lioness on the far side, the one with its head raised?

Martin: The one we saw near the lake the day before yesterday?

Me: No, that's the one with the scar.

Martin: I'm sure the one near the lake didn't have a scar.

Me: You're right. It didn't have a scar. The one on the far side doesn't have one either.

Martin: Well, it's moved now, anyway.

When you're seeing thirty or so lion every day this sort of thing can get tedious. So I began to give them names, or rather nicknames, since they already had 'official' Swahili names given by the scientists. The latter meant nothing to me I'm afraid. They might as well have had numbers attached to them. Whenever possible my names had some connection with a place, personal appearance, or a happening. So that there was

Hunters of the Plains

never any doubt about Munge Male No. 3. I called him 'Killer'. He had a ferocious temperament.

The names of the six resident prides – Seneto, Lake, Munge, Nomad, Tokitok, Gorigor – had been given by the Bygotts (see map). They were called after the locations which were their home territories. I was happy to stick to this but I did my own christening of individuals.

For example, there was a group of four lions, three maned males associating with a single female from the Nomad pride who were known officially to the SRI as Shababi, Shababa and Laiki; the female was Shabaki. Now that's a hell of a mouthful to remember, let alone to say when making a quick identification, perhaps talking, while bumping along, to your driver. My daughter Rebecca's favourite bedtime story was 'Goldilocks and the Three Bears'. So who else could this group of three boys and a girl be? I've never met anyone, however, who knows the names of the three bears themselves so I had to christen this trio something individually. The female was obviously Goldilocks. As a matter of fact it rather suited her. Her consorts I called, for reasons best known to myself at the time and now forgotten, Lock, Stock and Barrel.

Recognizing the individuals of the various prides was an essential first step, just as it had been with the members of the different hyena clans. It cut down the odds considerably when filming. If I could recognize a group at once and know whether they were within their own territory, I had some chance of guessing where they might hunt next.

However, what I really had to decide was which of the six prides would be the most profitable to stick with for filming purposes. The odds were that one would pay a bigger dividend than the others. But which? What I needed to do quickly was to sort out the pride most likely to hunt most often in daylight and in territory where I could film the action.

I have read somewhere that, statistically, the most effective lion hunting unit is two adult females operating together. I

The Lion

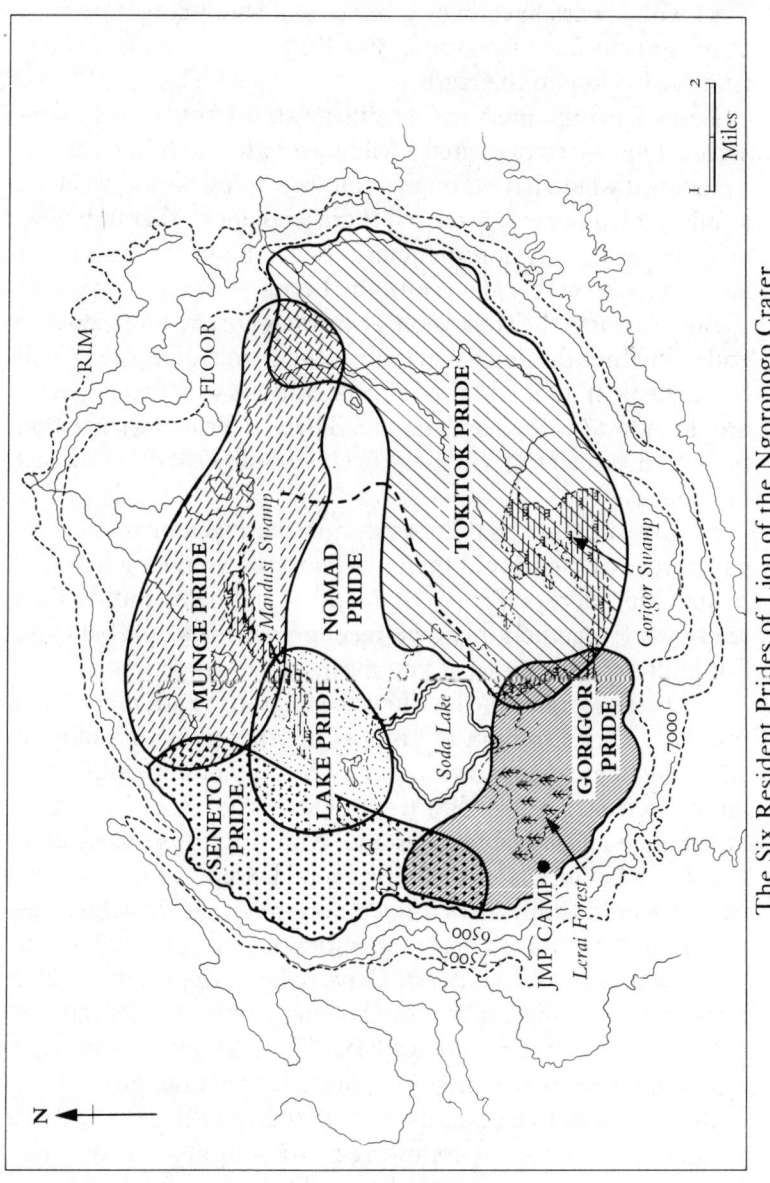

The Six Resident Prides of Lion of the Ngorongo Crater

think you always have to be a bit careful about accepting such statements at their face value, but I'd be surprised if this one isn't fairly close to the truth.

Lions have the most extraordinary ability to conceal themselves. I have seen one catch a wildebeest after stalking it across a plain you would have thought wouldn't hide a rabbit, let alone a fully grown lioness. Even so, there's no doubt that individually they are pretty conspicuous animals. So in that respect at any rate, the smaller the group the better.

But of course the stalk is only one phase of the hunt, not the end of it. Once the lion has actually caught hold of its prey it still has to hang on to it and this, presumably, is why two lionesses are thought to be better than one. There is far less chance that their intended victim will shake itself loose and escape at the last moment.

All this supposes that lionesses hunting together actually do co-operate. If they don't, then two lionesses would, on balance, be less, not more, effective than one on her own. But do they really work together? My own feeling is that they probably do but it all depends on what you mean by 'co-operation'.

Lions are social animals. They live in groups and, more often than not, they also hunt in groups. In other words a lion is an animal which, when hunting alongside another lion, must tend more often than not to find itself in an advantageous situation rather than a disadvantageous one. And since it is self-evident that to co-operate is of greater general advantage than otherwise, I would think that co-operation must, on the whole, be the order of the day. This co-operation may be of a high order but by the same token it doesn't have to be. As long as the lion is capable of keeping quiet, not showing itself, and is ready to rush in at the critical moment, that is all that is needed to ensure that two lionesses together are more effective than one.

But it doesn't necessarily follow that you'll get the best photographic results by following the best hunters. If they are hunting the same prey, two lions will need to hunt less frequently than a larger group. An adult male wildebeest weighs perhaps 350 pounds. Of this some 100 pounds consists of bone, hair, horns and so on, stuff that lion won't eat. So that leaves 250 pounds of meat to be shared between two animals who may stay with their kill for perhaps a day and a half. By contrast, 10 lions will polish off 250 pounds of meat in no more than 4 or 5 hours. At the end of that time it's true that they will then go off and sleep, but nevertheless at that point they are already at the start of their next hunting cycle, whereas the two lionesses have at least one more day to go before they reach a similar stage.

So, ideally, what I sought was a group of young lion. Youngsters don't have the experience and therefore have to try more frequently. I needed rather more than two or three since numbers are another factor that will help to move things along and produce frequent kills. One such group was known to the Bygotts, and consequently to me, as the 'Tokitok Seven'.

The Tokitok Pride took their name from the Oloitokitok Springs which were the most prominent land feature within their territory. At the end of 1977 the total pride consisted of thirty-two animals that we could recognize. There was another group that went around together from the same pride and these I shall call the Tokitok Ten. In addition to the Ten and the Seven there were three old males, Fred, Frodo and Frog and two smaller groups of females each accompanied by fairly small cubs.

When I'd decided on the characteristics of the group I wanted, I consulted David and Jeanette Bygott's notes. The other main candidates for consideration as stars were Goldilocks and Co., the Lake Pride and the Tokitok Ten.

The Lake Pride operated close to my camp. This would have been an advantage in terms of time-saving, but their territory was criss-crossed by a series of reed-filled *korongos*, or *guthos*, much favoured by the pride and in which they were extremely difficult to locate.

The Goldilocks outfit weren't much of a proposition either. I couldn't see them having much success in daylight since the Three Bears were far too conspicuous. Finally there was the Tokitok Ten. Early on we had seen this pride hunting in daylight and, indeed, had experienced two agonizing near misses in their company. But they were just a little too unwieldy for my liking. When they were on the move, their six almost fully grown males lumbered along behind the lionesses, occasionally stopping to sit down and scratch, leaping playfully onto each other, striding side by side, tails held high, moving across the plains with all the grace and subtlety of an armoured regiment. I felt that what I needed was a group with rather more chance of success in daylight than this and, according to the Bygotts' notes, the Tokitok Seven seemed to be it.

At this early stage I must admit that I had never, to the best of my knowledge, seen the Tokitok Seven in action and even now I can not say that I deliberately went out to look for them. You set out in the morning and look around and if you come across a situation that looks promising the thing to do is stick with it. You don't go charging off in search of something you may never find. A lion in the bush is the equivalent of a bird in the hand. And even when we found them the circumstances were such that it was some time before I realized exactly what we had got.

Boxing Day morning started overcast. We left camp at 5.45 a.m. and drove across the Crater towards a favourite lookout, Enkitati Hill. Once on top I opened the forward hatch and stood up to look round. It had rained heavily over the previous two days and the ground below was a mass of pools that shone silver as the sun struggled to penetrate a confused layer of mist and low cloud.

Back the way we had come, one of the maned Munge males plodded through the mud, heading away from the lake shore. Behind him followed five other lion that I couldn't identify at that distance. Then, to my left, a lion roared. I swung the binoculars on their mount until they were about lined up with the sound and then peered through them. There was the

The Lion

Nomad group just leaving a carcass around which some thirty hyena were gathered. Most likely it was a kill they had made themselves and which lion had scavenged.

There didn't seem much point in following the Nomads so I continued my slow scan of the central plains. The outlook was dismal. The ground was sodden and small groups of animals either stood around or picked their way gingerly between the puddles. Then, far off, just visible in the mist, I spotted two groups of hyenas. They were circulating around a series of confused shapes that looked as if they might be lions.

We left Enkitati and made our way to the Scratching Rocks hillock. The vague shapes were indeed lion. There were two groups of them. Two females, accompanied by 2 young cubs lay on their own a short distance from 7 other lions, 3 females and 4 males, not yet fully grown it's true, but large and powerful animals for all that. The larger of the two parties was finishing off the remains of a dead wildebeest. But from the blood-stained appearance of at least one of the hyena it looked as if this too was a carcass the lions had stolen.

It was obvious that the hyena thought the lions were about to depart for they were calling continuously using the low, rather mournful tone that hyena seem to reserve exclusively for situations of this sort. It seems as if they are trying to unnerve the lions into leaving rather earlier than they otherwise might have done, although I have yet to see a lion that showed any sign of being intimidated by this display. It was a situation I had already filmed on a number of occasions and since there didn't seem to be any point in covering it yet again, I left the movie camera on it's tray behind me and reached for the Nikon.

I had taken several stills of the goings-on when the action began to slacken. The hyena, apparently realizing that their psychological warfare wasn't having the desired affect, stood around ineffectually. I lowered the camera and looked up. There, to my surprise, since I certainly hadn't been aware of her approach, I saw a solitary buffalo cow standing perhaps 200

Hunters of the Plains

yards away. For a while she remained motionless, head held high. Then, for no very obvious reason, she charged full tilt at three of the lionesses that had already left the carcass and were lying together a little way off quietly minding their own business. As the buffalo approached, they scattered. I kept my still camera on the buffalo, expecting it to go straight on through. Instead though, it stopped, wheeled round and began to run back the way it had come.

Up to the point when the buffalo turned it wasn't really a situation worth filming. After all, what can you do with 20 or 30 feet of film showing a buffalo running across the plains? In turning, though, it lost all it's momentum and there, for a few seconds, it remained, travelling very slowly indeed, in close proximity to the three lionesses. In a flash, one of them was on the buffalo's back. I dropped the Nikon and grabbed the Arriflex movie camera. I had it loaded with high-speed film and the speed already set to give me slow-motion. I slid the camera onto its mount, plugged it into the panel and ran the motor. There was the buffalo in the viewfinder. Quickly I focussed and reached for the aperture ring to set the f. stop. Nothing! I rotated the control a couple of times. But still nothing. I couldn't set the exposure. It had somehow jammed.

The buffalo collapsed under the combined weight of seven lions and breathed its last after only a short struggle. Quite often, when lion kill a buffalo the proceedings are drawn out and very messy. Not the sort of thing you can show on television at any length. But this was a good clean, merciful kill, in reasonable light and at close range, right out in the open and I didn't get so much as a foot of film out of it.

Of course, you could say 'Well, how could you expect lions that were just finishing off one meal to go after another straight away?' True. 'And who could have anticipated the arrival of the buffalo or that it would behave as foolishly as it did?' Equally true. But if I had done what I ought to have done and checked the functioning of the camera when we first stopped I would have located the fault. It would have taken me about one minute to put it right, and I would have got that kill and saved myself an awful lot of time and trouble later on trying to get another.

I sat there in a sort of numbed daze while the lions began to eat. Two of the lionesses that had been sitting some way off and had taken no part in the kill now approached with their cubs. One halted at a distance of 10 feet or so but the other came right up to the carcass and began to chew on the hindquarters. At this, two of the lionesses at the other end of the kill, bolted. Although I knew that the newcomers were Tokitoks all right, it was obvious they weren't regular members of this particular group. It was equally obvious from the mathematics of the situation that we had at last located what we'd been searching for . . . the Tokitok Seven. At that moment, I thought they were the answer to a cameraman's prayer.

In those first days of attempting to film lion hunting and killing, we tried a number of different methods. For a while we favoured the use of certain vantage points from which we could scan large areas of the Crater floor. The trouble with that system was that, although we never failed to locate large numbers of lion, the ones we saw usually weren't animals that were hunting. They were most frequently from groups that had killed and were now lying out in the sun, sleeping it off. The lions we badly needed just refused to show themselves.

Next we tried staying with various individual groups. We would drive around and locate a bunch of lions that didn't look as if they had eaten for some while. Then we would stick with them in the hope that if they killed in daylight we would be there. That wasn't too successful either.

We would spend a whole day sitting alongside a group of sleeping lions and nothing would happen. Around dusk they would get up and move off. We would follow as long as possible in order to try and establish the direction in which they were moving and when it was too dark to see them any longer we would push off back to camp. Next morning we would be up early. Inevitably they weren't where we thought they were. And when we did locate them there they were lying around with stomachs bulging.

But lions *were* killing in daylight. We kept on seeing the results of their work. So then we started driving round in a purely random fashion, hoping that by covering a lot of ground we would stand more chance of running into the sort of action we were looking for. I began to keep a log of 'Near Misses', in the hope that this might reveal where we were going wrong and show how we could put things right. As a wildlife cameraman I've always kept detailed records of incidents from which I felt I could learn something afterwards. Some of the entries I now consulted took place before I started out on the *Hunters* Special but they all told me something about the problems I was now facing.

Serengeti 1976
I don't know now quite why I stopped to watch them. I was on my way to Seronera one evening when I saw a bunch of lion lying together watching a wildebeest. They were doing so in a rather casual manner. After no more than a couple of minutes one lioness got up and walked off in a wide arc. She was obviously serious because of the low, crouching attitude she adopted. Once she was in position, a second lioness rose and made straight for the wildebeest which was grazing with its head facing away from the lioness at an angle of about 45 degrees. Slowly the lioness crawled towards it. At intervals the wildebeest raised its head briefly and took a quick look round. But on each of these occasions the lioness was stationary and did not attract the wildebeest's attention. This was just as well since the grass it was crawling through was no more than 6 inches high. The lioness moved closer and closer. All the other lion remained dead still. At the last minute the wildebeest, apparently getting an inkling that mischief was afoot, looked up, glanced around and started to run. The lioness moved towards

him as if propelled by springs. Two bounds and they went over together in a cloud of dust. We started up and rushed towards the struggle. As the dust began to clear I could see that the lioness had the wildebeest by the muzzle and was holding on with its forelegs off the ground like a dog tugging at a newspaper offered it in play. Suddenly the wildebeest seemed to flip over onto its back as if some invisible hand had swept its feet from under it. Immediately the lioness shifted her grip to its throat and within seconds the first of her relatives were onto it, ripping at its belly.

The suspense was almost unendurable. I simply couldn't believe that an animal the size of a lioness could approach an animal as alert as a wildebeest across several hundred feet of absolutely flat, open plain and grab hold of it in this way. And over the last few feet of the stalk I was willing the wildebeest to move saying to myself: 'Run, run . . .' but I'm not sure even at the last moment that it really saw anything.
Lesson: Lion can hide in any sort of cover. Never dismiss the least likely looking situation.

Mara River 1976
We were out one evening looking for hyena. Our camp was situated on the banks of the Mara. A short distance back from the river was a swamp. Along the intervening strip of ground was what we called a hyena alley. At night that strip came alive with hyena. Ngorongoro had nothing on the Mara for sheer weight of hyena numbers. That night, though, before we could get out into the mainstream of activity, we came on two large maned lions, characters we had seen around that area on a number of occasions before.

They were lying on an anthill when we first saw them but at our approach got up and ambled off across hyena alley in the direction of the swamp. After a while they came to a hole, sniffed around it for a while and then moved on. But the next burrow they discovered was somehow different. They sniffed long and hard at the various entrances until they were sure which if them was occupied. Then one of the pair very carefully and deliberately put a paw in and hooked out a wart-hog, just like a cat pawing a mouse. The second it came above ground the other male had its hindquarters clamped firmly in its jaws. This enabled its pal to get a similar hold on its head. The lion at the rear then proceeded to eat its way forward and both munched their way toward each other in a very amicable fashion with none of the spitting and snarling you normally see around a lion kill.

The whole operation was conducted with such speed and efficiency. I must admit that I had the decided impression that the two lions had done it all many times before. People often say that the large males are too big and clumsy to hunt effectively and must depend on the pride lionesses to do this for them. This doesn't always make sense. Males are often attached to a female group, but just as often they are nomadic, roaming singly or in small groups. While they may not be as good at hunting as the females, at least they must be as good as they need to be or they simply wouldn't survive.

Perhaps fishing in holes for wart-hog, antbear and such-like is a method of hunting especially favoured by male lions. It certainly needs more strength than speed. *Survival* is sending out an Image-Intensifier which enables one to shoot at night. I shall certainly watch nomadic Ngorongoro males to see if I can't get something similar after darkness.

Amboseli 1976
It is late one afternoon. We drive out of camp along the edge of the forest. After no more than a quarter of a mile we come round a corner and there is a group of wildebeest feeding in a small open glade. From behind a bush to the left, first one, then two lionesses appear. They crawl down the track towards us on their bellies, heads turned towards the wildebeest. Suddenly one gets up and runs round the next bush. There is a tremendous

The Lion

commotion as the wildebeest stampede. I couldn't say afterwards exactly what had happened, but I got the impression that the first lioness had run full-tilt into a wildebeest walking in the opposite direction. The wildebeest swerved to avoid it and was pulled down as it did so.

So often the action takes place with such speed that afterwards you aren't quite sure exactly what did happen. It was obvious that I should use a good deal of slow-motion in *Hunters* to record what went on. One function of the wildlife documentary is to give the audience a greater insight into what is happening than it could have gained even if present at the actual event. In the case of predators in action there is really only one way to do this – to slow the whole process down as much as possible. But to do that you've got to be ready before the event happens.

At this point my log of near misses comes right up to date with the recent frustrations experienced on *Hunters*.

Serengeti – 28.10.77
Returning from Day 1 of the Predator Census we were driving along the Ngare Nanyuki track making for Seronera. At about 11 o'clock Rebecca spotted some lions close to the road. We stopped to look at them. There were 3 adult females and 8 cubs of assorted sizes. All of them looked thin and in poor condition.

Within a very few minutes one lioness, which had been staring intently at three wart-hogs feeding perhaps 200 yards away, rose and moved off towards them along a bush-covered drainage line. The lioness paused and looked back towards the group, moved a few yards and then looked back again. At this, another lioness also got up. She started off in the opposite direction. Finally lioness number three joined in. Crouching low, she made directly towards the target. The cubs stayed put.

I think lionesses one and three got there first, but I can't be sure about this. At any rate, the wart-hog's end appeared to come quickly and there was none of the usual screaming which always horrifies me. The wretched animal disappeared under an avalanche of lion. The usual spitting and snarling match developed but as far as I could see everyone got something. Even a large wart-hog won't go far amongst eleven hungry lions.

Reason for miss: Left camera equipment in camp due to participation in SRI Predator Count.

Moral: Don't leave equipment behind for whatever reason!

Ngorongoro – 9.11.77

Around mid-day we found a newly-born Thomson's gazelle. It was with its mother, who let us get very close. I filmed her cleaning it, and the fawn feeding from her and exercising its legs. Eventually one of the Lakeside hyena clan appeared. The mother made off and left her offspring 'frozen' in the grass. The hyena walked past and I was able to go back after a suitable interval and film the baby still crouched in its clump of grass. By the time I had finished this it was about 2 o'clock, not a very productive time of day out on the plains. I decided to return to camp as there were things I needed to do there.

At five we left camp again, heading for the Lakeside hyena's communal den where I planned to spend the late afternoon filming young hyena at play. We re-traced our steps, crossing the Munge River at the point where it empties into the lake. Just ahead of us, from that position, we spotted six lions. They were the Lake Pride and they were eating an adult wildebeest. It looked as if they had been hiding in one of several large clumps of grass nearby and had ambushed their victim some time between two-thirty and four-thirty. The wildebeest could have died there and they might have scavenged it I suppose. But it certainly wasn't a hyena kill. Although quite close to the Lakesider's den, not one hyena was in sight nearby although several were lying around just out of sight. Nor were they present when we passed that way again heading back for camp at six-thirty.

Moral: Of course you don't get pictures of lion killing by sitting in camp. But by the same token, even if we had been out and about, it is unlikely that we would have been in the right place to film this kill. All I can say is that when passing through the Lake Pride territory, I shall always check those clumps of grass in case there are lion lying in wait.

Ngorongoro – 16.11.77

Left camp at 6 a.m. bound for Enkitati. Just short of the road that descends into the Crater I noticed a wildebeest running between us and the lake. Stopping for a closer look, we made out a lioness lying by the spring and another nearer the track. We pulled off the road to observe what was going on. The two lionesses lay still for some time and then, shortly after sunrise, both got up and walked across to an isolated patch of grass from the depths of which only their heads could be seen as they occasionally sat up and looked around.

After about 15 minutes a small herd of zebra filed past perhaps thirty yards away, apparently unaware of the lion's presence. Once past the clump, though, two suddenly stopped and looked back. Although they gave no audible warning, their attitude alerted the next group which, if they had held to their original course, would certainly have passed much closer to the lionesses.

Finally, one zebra either saw or smelled lion. It called with a creaky intake of breath immediately followed by a loud snort. Almost every zebra in a mixed herd of zebra and wildebeest grazing perhaps a quarter of a mile away raised their heads but very few of the wildebeest did. So this was interesting since such formations are supposed to be mutually advantageous.

It may be that this level of alarm was just about on the threshold at which wildebeest take notice of zebra signals. Be that as it may, from that point on the game was up. Almost as if they realized this, the two lionesses then left their hiding place. En route they were joined by a large, maned male who emerged from the rocks and walked rapidly towards them. When they met he stood with tail raised while one lioness sniffed him. Neither rubbed up against him so I presumed that he may well have been one of the six Munge males, known to them but not yet all that familiar.

After a short while the lionesses moved on. The male lay down. But when the females had almost reached the shade of a tree nearby, a second male appeared and headed towards the females. At this point the original male decided that the lionesses were a lot more attractive than he had first realized and came running up towards the tree. The lionesses lay down in the shade. Both males scratched at the ground and marked. Then they too lay down and that was the end of that.

Reason for miss: Lion discovered by zebra.

Moral: Apart form the actual charge and capture of the prey, the additional action that would obviously have been worth filming would have been the arrival of the males. I was unaware of their presence until afterwards. In future, take a very good look around if circumstances permit, so as to become aware of any other lion in the area.

Ngorongoro – 21.11.77

We descended from Enkitati around 11 a.m. after having spent some while on top searching for lion through the binoculars. Just past the junction of the Enkitati track and the main track, Martin suddenly pulled up. There in thick grass alongside us a lioness is crouched.

To our left the grass is very short and very green, just growing up on a large burned area. On the right where there was no burn there is an old growth, perhaps 2 feet tall, and it is this in which the lioness is lying crouched. The following is the situation.

There are two groups of wildebeest standing, feeding. One is staring in the general direction of the lioness.

At 10.30 some zebra walk off towards the swamp, other zebra begin slowly moving towards the lioness.

The Lion

Two golden jackals are paying a lot of attention to a patch of ground at the base of Enkitati. We have retreated up the slope again so that we have a better view and can see a Thomson's gazelle female hanging around nearby so she probably has a *toto*, a fawn, hidden in the grass there somewhere. Since there is very little cover it is lucky to escape the jackal which eventually give up and walk off. It is probably even luckier to escape the lion since it soon joins its mother. The pair walk slowly past the clump of grass in which the lioness is hidden.

I follow the action with my finger on the button only to discover that the diaphragm is not working. It takes me 5 minutes to remove the bloody lens and sort things out. I would have looked a bit silly if the lioness had charged out and taken the gazelle.

The wildebeest start moving towards the lioness in earnest. We drive down the hill to a more favourable position and can see the lioness' head peering out from the grass so we are ideally situated from every point of view. The weather is fine. The equipment is serviceable. We know the position of the lioness. The zebra are approaching.

The first few wildebeest pass a little too far out. Then some zebra arrive. Much closer now. One stops and looks at the grass. Two stop. Three. This doesn't affect the rest though. They graze closer and closer. Heads down. I keep my finger on the button. More zebra arrive. Still the lioness makes no move. But now the zebra mill around uneasily. For some reason they are disturbed, but it seems obvious that they are unaware of the lioness so close at hand or they wouldn't be where they are.

Finally, a small group moves closer, giving alarm calls. They still can't see anything but they know something is there. All this time a foal grazes close by, unmoved by all the fuss. At 2.55 they all move off. We have spent $4\frac{1}{2}$ hours for nothing more than a few feet of prey reactions.

Reason for miss: Lion discovered by zebra.
Future action: Nothing that I can think of!

Hunters of the Plains

Ngorongoro – 25.11.77

At 10 a.m. we were sitting on the Scratching Rocks hillock when Martin spotted some lion in the direction of Enkitati. We drove over and found they were part of the Tokitok Pride although they were in the Munge Pride's territory. There were 3 adult lionesses, 1 sub-adult female and 6 sub-adult males. Since they all looked a bit thin we decided to stay with them for a while.

At about 11 o'clock a storm began to brew up over Silali. It grew dark and there were several thunderclaps, which made a couple of the young males start visibly. At 11.30 the storm hit us and we were enveloped in a thick grey mist. The rain hammered down and water began to pour into the Land Rover. By this time I had brought all the gear in and put on the side screen but this made little difference to the water entering the car and so we started up and turned into the wind.

Outside, the lion huddled together, their backs to the wind. They looked thoroughly miserable and suddenly seemed to have shrunk. Their coats had a silvery sheen as the rain rolled off them. Their eyes were tightly shut. I took some black and white stills of them.

Then, at about 2.15 the rain eased off slightly and one young male got up, stretched and shook himself vigorously. Immediately the others rose as well, as if they'd been thinking the same thing all along and the ten of them headed off towards the swamp. The adults walked sedately but the young males trotted side by side, their tails held high, pushing and jostling and batting each others hind legs.

When they reached the track that borders the Mandusi Swamp they turned right and plodded along it in single file. Soon the leading female stopped and started staring intently at a mixed herd of wildebeest and zebra that were grazing about 100 yards to their left. More wildebeest were approaching across the plains. It was still raining steadily and most of them seemed to be trudging along more or less regardless of their surroundings.

The Lion

One by one the cubs got the message and collapsed along the roadside. The leading female advanced into the high grass at the edge of the track and lay down. Another went on down the track for a further 50 yards. They all lay very still. Slowly the herd grazed nearer. I could see one lioness carefully inching her way into the long grass in the direction of the wildebeest.

I replaced the camera on its mount. Although it was still raining I reckoned I could just get an exposure if I re-rated the film at 32 ASA. I was in such a good position that it was worth a try. I ran a few feet of film through the camera on the wildebeest advancing and on the backs of lion's heads crouched all round in the grass. But then, half-way between the opposing forces, a reedbuck stood up. It had been crouched down all this time and up to that point I hadn't the faintest idea it was there. The reedbuck looked around and stared straight at the lioness crouched no more than feet from it. It froze but gave no alarm call. Not the slightest twitch disturbed its flanks. But slowly, very slowly, its tail rose until it arched onto its back, exposing the brilliant white fur on its under-surface.

An alarm signal to all! The nearest zebra immediately called in fright. At this a second reedbuck jumped up out of nowhere and, whistling loudly, bounded off. And that was the end of it. The lions all got to their feet. The young males started chasing each other after their period of enforced inactivity. The adult females relaxed, rolling around on their backs and that was the end of that particular incident.

Only comment unprintable!

Ngorongoro – 27.11.77
The group of ten Tokitok were lying sprawled out on the grass and we were sitting beside them in the Land Rover. Although the sun was bright a light rain was falling and behind us I could see both ends of a rainbow. Just above ground level a multitude of swifts darted amongst the singing clouds of insects brought out by the rain.

'Do you see those five zebra about half-way along Enkitati?' asked Martin.
'Not yet.'
'Just where we saw that cheetah the other day.'
I shifted the binoculars a fraction. 'Right, I've got them.'
'Well, there's a lioness just below them.'
I stared hard. After a while I saw what he was looking at. There *was* a lioness there. The slope of Enkitati is contoured by game trails at this point and in one of them I could just make out a shape flattened against the hillside. It looked within feet of the zebra. For a good 10 minutes it lay there while the animals grazed. Then one zebra raised its head. Just in front of it there was a slight gulley. It seemed to me to be trying to make up its mind which way to go round this for it was on a steep slope. After the heavy rain it must have been a very slippery surface for even a zebra's hooves to grip. Finally it decided. Instead of going on it turned its head to go back. At that moment, presumably realizing that it was then or never, the lioness broke from the cover of the game trail and rushed. The zebra fled. The lioness didn't come within feet of them.
Reason for miss: Lioness trying to run up a steep slope did so prematurely. I included this incident to show just how close it is possible for a predator to get to its prey and still miss unless everything is in its favour.

Ngorongoro – 27.11.77
After the heavy rain of the early afternoon, the Tokitok group is now sprawled out in the sun soaking up the warmth. The ten lions have already tried once for a wildebeest and now we sit alongside them not because I have any real hope that they will do anything more, but rather because I can't think of anything better to do.

Suddenly one female sits up and stares off towards the Mandusi Swamp. Her action brings the other two on their feet. As one they set off at a trot, heading towards the nearest reedbed. I turn towards the swamp and see in the distance a file of wildebeest coming through from the far side. One lioness goes right through the reeds and on into the open space beyond. Another stops in the reeds. The third turns sharp right and, crouching low, makes her way along it. I run the camera. She makes a magnificent sight in the last of the sunlight but its really a little too far away to be effective.

The wildebeest come on, apparently unaware of the ambush being laid for them. But their path takes them just too far away from the nearest lioness and she makes no move.

Comment: It would appear that lion that are hungry enough will not hesitate to hunt during the daytime and any situation in which they are lying in country which provides them with good cover is worth watching.

Final comment: I hope to God I've learned something from studying where and why it all went wrong. Maybe so, but I shall certainly need more than a little luck if it's ever to go right!

11
The Tokitok Ten

It wasn't all disaster, though. Even if I didn't get the lion kills I so desperately needed, I did get some wonderful interaction between lion and hyena. On 30 November, just after the last entry in my diary of near-misses, I witnessed and filmed the most extraordinary pitched battle.

The only lion we could find that didn't look so full of food that they were about to burst were the Tokitok Ten. They were lying in the long grass out on the central plains of the Crater and some of them looked positively bony. We watched them stalk two zebra. The females snaked their way through the grass, their presence given away by one of the sub-adult males, which sauntered along two or three hundred yards behind, as large as life and twice as visible. 'If they don't kill tonight,' we agreed, 'they'll be worth watching tomorrow.'

But the next morning the Tokitoks were nowhere to be seen. We searched high, we searched low. Old lion, young lion, males, females, lion we'd never even seen before, when I totted them up at midday we'd seen forty-one in all, but of the Tokitoks, there wasn't even the tip of a tail to be seen. Finally, at 2 o'clock we climbed to the top of Enkitati and there below us, on the near side of the Mandusi swamp, were all ten of them happily tucking in to not one but two freshly killed wildebeest. It was small consolation to see the wisdom of our course of action demonstrated in such emphatic terms. Near misses of this kind were getting to be the story of my life. Almost every day, or so it seemed at the time, I had arrived back in camp in the evening with a tale of how we had figured out what to do, only to arrive on the scene a few minutes too late.

As I sat there, gloomily wondering what to do next, Martin pointed out a herd of zebra crossing the swamp at a trot. This was not how zebra usually crossed so I reached for the glasses. Just as I got them focussed, the stallion bringing up the rear turned and charged full tilt at a hyena close on his heels. A little further to the left three more hyena were galloping across the plains. We came down from Enkitati at full tilt. Four hyena that had been hanging around the Tokitoks were running hard along the track ahead of us.

The zebra, some twenty-five or so, quite a big group, thundered across the road not far away. But where were their pursuers? We stopped and I climbed up through the hatch to look around. The hyena I had seen on their way through the swamp were jumping up and down trying to see what was happening above the tall grass. But the four hyena that had run down the track ahead of us had peeled off to the right and had gone after the zebra. I followed flat out.

Once again the stallion sorted them out. The herd had bunched up on Enkitati so that their right flank was protected by the rocky slope. Each time the hyena moved in, the stallion trotted down to meet them. It was an effective method of defence and the hyena soon gave up.

I was pretty certain that the reason why the first hyena group had stopped was because they had reached the edge of their territory or had at least penetrated as far into 'no man's land' as seemed wise under the circumstances. Maybe the presence of the four hyena already hovering around the Tokitoks had deterred them from going any further. But now another group of hyena was approaching from what I took to be Seneto territory.

They passed the hyena standing by the zebra at a run,

heading directly for the Tokitok kill. I don't think they were aware of this group but the latter certainly saw them for they too turned and plunged into the long grass.

By now, we had some experience of the confusion that would result when the three hyena groups met. So instead of following along behind we turned and climbed as far up Enkitati as we could. The Tokitoks were still in possession of their wildebeest. Around them the hyena prowled, still in separate groups. But across the Mandusi I could see other hyena hurrying to reach the scene. It was one of the few times I wished I had a bigger telephoto lens. From our position on the hillside we had a clear view of what was going on but were just a little too far away to be able to film. From down below we would be able to film alright, but there the action would be confused to say the least of it.

We drove off the hill and headed for the lion. Under the circumstances there wasn't much choice. It was the right decision though.

You know those old paintings of battles in which soldiers are depicted hacking and bludgeoning each other while only a few feet away something entirely inconsequential is going on. Three gunners are sitting in the shelter of a wagon playing cards. Well, it was a bit like that. Just ahead of us there was a small clump of grass. Throughout the episode, which must have lasted all of 20 minutes, there was never a moment when the grass didn't have its complement of hyena sniffing around it, scratching or greeting each other, apparently oblivious of the action going on all round, regardless of how hectic this became. It was a quiet oasis in the midst of all the excitement. Hyena from at least three clans were intermingling on all sides. A tremendous chase developed in which two groups went haring off down the swamp into Seneto territory and then swung east through the marsh and back into what I took to be Lakeside ground. At least twenty hyena left the scene as a result of that chase but there were plenty left and the racket they made was beyond belief.

Finally, even the lion could take it no longer. Apparently

startled by a particularly fiendish outburst, a group of them rose to their feet and scattered right across the path of a hyena who had the misfortune to be rushing past at that moment. In a flash one of the young males had him and he was pinned to the ground. He was lucky, that hyena. I think it was the fact the sub-adults got him that saved his bacon. They pawed at him and took tentative bites at his back as if they didn't really know what to do with their unexpected catch. And when they remained still for a few seconds he tucked his tail between his legs and came out from under them like a shot from a gun and got away with it.

Though I flirted with other prides it was, you will recall, with the Tokitok Seven that I had mainly decided to throw in my lot. It was the Seven I tried to follow whenever the situation seemed favourable. At last, in early January, I got lucky.

Martin and I spotted an eland surrounded by hyena. From the way she was circling and dodging it was obvious she was defending herself pretty desperately. I reckoned that even 8 or 10 hyena were fairly unlikely to tackle an antelope the size of a cow, unless, of course, she was already wounded or otherwise in trouble. So the likelihood was that the hyena were after her calf.

The action had only just started when we drove up and so I was able to film the gradual build-up of hyenas. The eland was doing pretty well, lowering her horns and jabbing at each attacker as it came in. But, of course, as usual she couldn't deal with them all. One hyena darted in and grabbed the calf, but somehow it managed to struggle free and back came its mother.

We were lucky about our position. We had managed to stop the Land Rover on a bank about 10 feet above the action, so the angle was a good one. I had a fully loaded 400 foot magazine on so I was able to run continuously. I was just thinking about taking my finger off the button when, ambling in from camera right, came a sub-adult male lion. I recognized him as Jesse James, one of our Tokitok Seven.

Jesse took over the situation from the hyena straight away. With a growl and a spit or two, he scattered them. But he reckoned without the mother who, if she didn't actually attack Jesse, looked as though she might at any moment.

At this Jesse James upped and charged her for about 30 yards. She lashed out with both rear feet and caught him with at least one hoof and with a noise like a big drum being beaten. Jesse was obviously put out by this and clawed at her hindquarters with both forepaws. However, he didn't follow up his attack because now the hyena had moved in on the calf again.

Jesse returned and chased them off and then settled down to enjoy his booty. The hyena hung around looking dispirited. A jackal or two were in there somewhere as well.

I concluded that the action must be over but happily kept the camera running. My knowledge of the Tokitok Seven suggested that the other six were around somewhere. Sure enough, within 20 seconds or so, a female (Hope I think it was) came trotting in from the same direction from which Jesse had approached. However, she apparently wasn't confident enough to try to share the kill and walked rather nervously past him.

Within seconds, though, another of the terrible Seven arrived on the scene. This was another sub-adult I called Buffalo Bill. He obviously wanted a share of the calf but wasn't quite sure how to go about it. Jesse was probably older than both the newcomers as he had a much more developed mane. So Bill sidled up and then threw himself down with his backside on the calf, right in Jesse's face. This was too much for Jesse James who picked the carcass up and trotted off smartly with it, 30 yards into the longer grass.

The drama wasn't over yet. Two other males arrived and disputed the dead eland calf, each grabbing a leg and a snarling, spitting tug-of-war resulted. At this the female, Hope, judged it safe to grab herself an eland steak. Finally there were four lions pulling and tugging at the carcass with the other three Tokitoks reclining hopefully in the grass nearby.

Bulls-eye, at last! Or, if not a bulls-eye, then what marksmen call a very good 'inner'. I was finally somewhere near the centre of the target.

The sequence which was covered from start to finish with the essential cutaways (shots that film editors must have to maintain continuity in cutting) demonstrated quite a few valuable aspects of lion and prey behaviour. Defence against hyena; successful evasion of lion attack by a large prey species; lion versus hyena and finally lion versus lion on a kill.

A few days later the Tokitok Seven gave me another valuable sequence which clearly demonstrated how ineffective lion are when making a long chase in the open.

This time the star was Hope, even though, as a star, she seemed cast in the role of tragedienne in that she never seemed to succeed. This time her failure was against a new-born wildebeest calf which she spotted in the open. Hope ran 200 yards across the plain to catch it. The calf was still fairly unsteady on its legs so that it couldn't follow its mother as fast as it should have done. This was what gave Hope the opportunity and seemed to her to make a long chase worthwhile. The cow saw her coming and tried to lead her offspring away, but the youngster suddenly got springs in its feet and left Hope standing, hopelessly pooped and wondering why she'd run out of steam.

I thought to myself that, after all this time filming lion, I knew exactly how she felt when cheated at a kill.

Heartening as their two recent performances were, and delighted as I was to have captured them on film, I realized only too well that both had only occurred because the Tokitok Seven were very young and inexperienced. This was why they had made such a fuss over one small calf. It was easy meat. Hope's lack of experience had made her pick on a newborn wildebeest and then fail to catch it. Equally it was this quality of inexperience that had lead me to pick the Seven as my stars in the first place. Now I began to wonder whether I had made the right choice.

Hunters of the Plains

There was a strong temptation to stay with them in the hope that they would perform again before long. Under other circumstances I would probably have done just that. But there were other factors that had to be taken into consideration.

I was aware when we began to follow them that the Tokitok Seven were not an ideal group. The only lions that would fit this description from my point of view would be a party that slept all night and hunted all day. But such a phenomenon certainly didn't exist in Ngorongoro and I doubt if it does anywhere. So I had been quite happy to settle for a bunch that I felt would give me at least something I could film. They had now done better than that. They had done me proud.

Their performance before the camera showed perfectly legitimate, if immature, lion tactics. In essence, all predators need to be opportunistic. The chance presents itself and must be seized, and in this respect the Seven were not found lacking. But what I now needed was something entirely different. Mind you, I wasn't knocking what I'd got. But I was after all, trying to produce a Special and what I needed to show was not just the lion's ability to seize an opportunity, but also its ability to create one. In this respect, the trouble with the Tokitok Seven lay in the fact that they had no experienced lioness with them whose actions they could copy. Being able to learn from one's elders is one of the principle advantages of a social existence. The young lionesses go hunting with their elders and, by watching them at work, learn their craft. By contrast, the Seven simply lay around waiting either for some animal to blunder into them, or for a hyena kill they could rob. Looking at them I often wondered how such a group would have fared out on the plains to the east where the density of hyena wasn't so high. It wouldn't have surprised me if they had starved.

Earlier on in this story you may remember that I referred to the protective 'bubble' that surrounds every member of the prey species and how, to some degree, the extent to which a predator can disregard the bubble is an indication of its effectiveness as a hunter. Measured by this yardstick, wild dogs must be very effective indeed, since they simply don't bother to conceal themselves. They walk up to a herd of wildebeest very slowly. Then, when they are close enough, they rush forward. The wildebeest panic. But instead of attempting to press home their attack straight away they either stop and watch or just cruise alongside the stampede attempting to select a victim before really shifting into top gear. Lion can't do this. They don't have the speed, stamina or manoeuvreability that's required for these tactics to pay off. So, because they are such large and conspicuous animals, they have developed an almost uncanny ability to conceal themselves.

For *Hunters*, I just had to show a lioness stalking during the daytime. Although this wouldn't be entirely typical, I felt that in many ways it would be more impressive. So now I decided to ditch the Seven. But which pride should I choose and where could I find a group that would be both active in daylight *and* sufficiently skilled to stand a reasonable chance of success?

Within the huge Tokitok Pride itself there were two small groups of females with cubs who obviously had to be competent hunters. But I didn't favour these particular animals as, rightly or wrongly, I felt they would be unlikely to leave their cubs when we were around and so our very presence might tend to inhibit just the type of activity we had come to cover.

The other main Tokitok group, the Tokitok Ten, had lionesses with them alright, but their six large sub-adult males were so conspicuous it was difficult to believe they would ever have much success in daylight. So what did that leave?

Goldilocks and the Three Bears were also non-starters because Goldilocks herself had gone missing now and I was reasonably certain that Lock, Stock and Barrel, left to their own devices, would spend most of their time scavenging from hyena.

I wasn't too keen on the Munge Pride either since I knew very little about them at this stage and wasn't anxious to start work

Hunters of the Plains

all over again with a bunch of complete strangers. That left the Lake Pride and the Gorigors. Under other circumstances I believe I would have gone for the Lake Pride since their territory offered good cover for daytime stalking. But at that time they were being accompanied by at least two of the big Munge males and that was as much of a drawback as anything.

So in the end, I came down in favour of the Gorigor girls.

The Gorigor Pride territory extended from the road down from the Crater rim in the far west to the fringes of the Gorigor swamp in the east. We had seen them further afield than this a couple of times. During November when so many of the wildebeest and zebra had moved across to Enkitati, they had begun to encroach on Lake Pride territory to quite a noticeable extent. Now, though, they had retreated from around the mouth of the Munge and were concentrated in the hills between the west end of the Lerai Forest and the Seneto Swamp.

There were twelve of them that I knew about: 2 young males and 10 females of varying ages.

At the beginning of February they appeared to be having a pretty hard time of it. At the eastern end of their range there was a marked absence of either wildebeest or zebra and this had forced them to concentrate in a small area not far west of our camp. Here, although there were plenty of animals around during the day, there was a definite exodus every evening. Between about 6 and 7 o'clock, long files of animals formed up, and, descending the slight slope below the Seneto Spring, trudged across the mud flats into the comparative safety of Lake Pride territory. Similarly, every morning, there was a mass movement back again.

That the Gorigor lion weren't having much success, either by day or by night, was suggested by their condition. All were lean and boney. The younger of the two males in particular looked like a horror picture from some famine relief appeal, so much so that I called him 'The Refugee'. One of the females was recovering from some mishap and was in exceptionally poor shape.

Either she had tackled something too hot for her to handle properly or she had been in a fight with another lioness. About three-quarters of the way down her back she had a very large open wound that was only just beginning to heal. In comparison with the Tokitok Seven, they were a very flea-bitten looking bunch indeed. But regardless of what they looked like, their circumstances seemed such that daylight hunting was at least a reasonable possibility. And so we decided to give them a go.

The first day that we spent exclusively with the Gorigors was 5 February. When we had been filming the Seven, I used to leave camp just before six and we would pass through the hills I called the Himalayas when it was still dark. Now, though, we were able to take a blissful 15 minutes extra in bed in order not to arrive in Gorigor land too early.

We cruised slowly along the track. Not 100 yards from the Lerai Forest, Der Fuhrer, the older of the two Gorigor males, was wandering along in company with a female I couldn't identify. We stopped to watch. After a while it became clear they were following a scent trail and, sure enough, when I turned to see where it was leading them, there were three other females we hadn't noticed. The lionesses greeted each other by rubbing heads. Der Fuhrer didn't deign to make contact with the girls but settled himself instead on a nearby ridge and gazed majestically about him.

For once I felt optimistic. I somehow believed the Gorigors were likely to give us the one full-blooded, daylight kill that I still needed. And when I'd got that, there only remained the cheetah hunts to be tackled. . . .

Epilogue

John began to shoot footage on the Gorigor Pride and indeed it looked as though they might live up to his expectations.

One morning, 3 weeks after the account of his first day with the Gorigors was written, he got up as usual at 5.45 to make tea before he set out to find his lion.

Jenny Pearson heard him leave the tent. Almost at once there was a shot. She heard John call out: 'What the bloody hell goes on?' Immediately there were two more shots, the first of which struck John in the forehead, killing him instantly. The other hit a tree.

What had happened was this. The game guard attached to camp by the Conservation Authority had heard Maasai shouts and cow bells. In fact, these were perfectly normal sounds made by Maasai herdsmen driving cattle down to water over the Crater rim. The young game guard, who was plainly terrified by the reputation of the Maasai camp raiders, panicked, imagining that they were about to attack the camp. The measure of his panic and the desperately random nature of the accident can be judged by the fact that he fired all three shots from *inside* his tent. John Pearson was carrying a torch at the time and it is thought that he probably shone this in the direction of the first shot when he called out to know what was happening. The second and fatal shot must have been fired in the general direction of the torch.

Epilogue

The game guard immediately placed himself under close arrest and was shortly afterwards taken away by the Conservation Authorities. It is not known what happened to him. Jenny Pearson returned to England with Rebecca but is back working in Tanzania at the moment of writing.

The missing cheetah sequence for *Hunters* was shot by one of John's *Survival* colleagues in Africa, Bob Campbell. But *Hunters of the Plains* remains John Pearson's film.

This book is John's too. All I have done is to edit and organize that suitcase full of notes that Jenny brought back with her to England.

Colin Willock

Index

Bold figures denote main sections; P. stands for John Pearson

Aerial recces., 23, 27–9, 36–7
Africa, x, 2, 8, 69, 109
  East, 7, 14, 19, 27, 36, 60, 93, 97
  E. African Community, 111
  conservationists in, 56
Airways, E. African, ix; P. as pilot, 4, 6–8, 14, 18, 37
Amboseli, 96, 102, 103, 146
Angata Kiti Pass, 40, 55, 73
Anjari, Inayat, 50–2
antbears, 146
antelope *see* eland, gazelle, wildebeest
anthropologists, 38–9
archaeologists, 60
Arusha, 40, 108, 110–13, 116

BBC-Time-Life, 96
bomas (Maasai), 61, 63, 64
buffalo, 141–2
Bygott, Drs. D. & J., 123, 130, 131, 135, 136, 139

Caldera (crater), 121
cats (domestic), 94
cheetahs: **94–105**; x, 1, 22, 23, 30, 33, 34, 60, 106, 114, 115–16, 118–19, 134, 165, 167; 'Violet Mary', 95, 99–103
conservation, 56, 60, 93–5, 121
Conservation Area HQ, Ngorongoro, 35, 70, 72, 108, 116, 122, 166–7
Crater Highlands, Tanzania, 107, 121
Customs Service, 111–13

Dar-es-Salaam, 90, 91, 97
David, driver to P., 47, 54, 58–9, 62–74 *passim*, 81, 116
dogs (domestic), 94
dogs (hunting): **35–92**; x, 1, 26–8, 30, 33; litters, 35–6; 37, 42–3; packs, 44; 55, 60, 76–9, 80–2; rituals, 83; 100, 106, 114, 134, 163; *see also* Genghis Pack
donkeys (Maasai), 54, 57, 60, 63

Eland, 122, 159
Enkitati, 118, 121, 127, 128, 130, 140–1, 149–152 *passim* 154, 156–8, 164
Entebbe, 8
Eternal Triangle (film) x, 37, 106–7
Ethiopia, x

Index

Filming (wildlife): **1–13**; approach to, xii, **26–33**; of birds, ix, 5, 6, 12, 58; 17, 41, 42–3, 46–7, 55, 69, 76–7, 82, 84, 89–90, 93, 95–103, 107, 119–20, 125–6, 129–30, 138–44, 147–155; *see also Hunters of the Plains* (film)
flamingoes, ix, 32–3, 121
Frame, George, 114, 116
Frankfurt Zoo, x

Game guards, 116–17, 122, 166–7
Game Parks, 8, 17, 97
gazelles, 33, 36, 56, 58, 83, 89, 91, 99, 122
    Thomsons, 28, 33–4, 50, 88, 107, 119, 151
Geertsema, 'Inky', 40, 45, 52, 53, 69, 70, 80, 97
Genghis Pack, 40–5, 47, 53–7, 69, 74–7, 80; killing, 81–8; 89–90, 106, 116
    Homer, 40–1, 45–6, 82, 86–7, 89–92
    Jinja, 40–1, 45–6, 82, 86–7, 89–92
    Kali, 40–1, 44–6, 54; litter, **75–92**; 82, 88, 91–2
    Marcus, 40–1, 43–6, 54, 69, 74, 77, 80, 82, 86–92
geology, 38–9, 121
giraffes, 80
goats (Maasai), 60, 64
Gol Mountains, 38–40, 55, 57, 61–2, 68–9
Gorigor swamp, 164
Grose, Peter, x
Grzimek, Dr. Bernhard, x

Hippopotamus, 9
hunters, 9–11
Hunters of the Plains (film) xi, 1–33 *passim*, 41, 58, 94, 105–6, 116, 122, 133–4, 144, 147, 163–7
hyenas: **121–133**; 1, 28, 30, 32–3, 74–6, 81, 88–9, 104, 114, 134, 140–1, 145, 156–60, 162–3
    clans: Lakeside, 126–7, 129, 158
    Scratching Rocks, 126–9
    Seneto, 131, 157–8

Impala, 94
Innocent Killers (H. & J. van Lawick), 43 & n illustrations, vii, viii

Jackals, 30; golden, 107–8, 151; silver, 131, 160
Japanese, vehicles, 19, 20

Kasese, 8, 9
Kenya, 7, 19, 36–7, 68, 95, 96, 109, 111
Kerimasi, volcano, 39, 40
Kilimanjaro, 101
Kruuk, Hans, 123, 126

Lake Lgarya, 35, 49, 98
Lake Magadi, ix, 9
Lake Manyara, 109, 113
Lake Marzak, 49, 52, 98
Lake Rukwa, 9
Lake Victoria, 97
Lawick, H. & J. van, 12, 40; *Innocent Killers*, 43 & n
leopards, 13, 30, 60, 94
Lemuta, 55, 57, 73, 81, 88

Index

Lerai forest, 121, 164, 165
lions: **134–165**; 1, 10, 23, 30; and prides, 44; and donkey, 54, 57, 60; and Maasai, 61, 67–8; 94, 104–6, 114–15, 122–3, 130; hunting, 137–9, 144–6, 161–3
   Prides: Gorigor, 136, 164–6
   Lake, 136, 139, 164
   Munge, 131–3, 135–6, 140, 150, 152, 163–4
   Nomad, 136, 141
   Seneto, 136
   Tokitok Seven, 139–40, 143, 152, 159–63, 165
   Tokitok Ten, 130, 139, 153, 154, **156–9**
lizards, and jackals, 108

Maasai: **56–74**; 40, 47, 54–5, 88, 116–17, 118–19, 122, 166
Maasailand, 64, 122
Malcolm, James, 115
Mara River, 76, 145
Martin, driver to P., 116–17, 124, 132, 150, 152, 154, 157, 159
Mandusi swamp, 118, 130, 152, 154, 156, 158
maps, 48, 137
Mathenge, cook to P. 61, 62, 67
mishaps, on safari, **47–56**
Mlanje Depression, 70
Munge River, 118, 121, 135, 164

Naabi Hill, Serengeti, 27, 45, 76
Nairobi, 30, 37, 108, 109, 110, 111
   Airport, 4, 9
Namanga, Customs Post, 109, 111, 112

Nasera Rock, 40, 57, 60, 61, 73
Ndutu Safari Lodge, 35–7, 40–1, 45, 47, 49–53, 55, 72–3, 97, 103, 106–8, 112–17
Ngare Nanyuki track, 147
Ngorongoro, Tanzania, 37, 49, 51, 52, 66, 69, 70, 119, 145–6, 162
   Conservation Authority, *see under* Conservation
   Crater, xi, 9, 39, 105–8, 114–18, 121–3, 128, 134, 143, 156, 164, 166; camp in, 148–150, 152–4
   Safari Lodge, 108–9
   Range, 38, 39

Ol Babbal, 39
Olduvai Gorge, 9, 37–9, 49, 97
Oloitokitok Springs, 139
ostrich, eggs of, 12, 13

Pearson, John, author & photographer, ix–xi, 166–7
Pearson, Jenny, wife of P., x, xi, 15–17, 23, 37, 108, 113, 116, 122, 166–7
   Rebecca, daughter of P., 15–17, 114, 117, 122, 136, 147, 167
pelicans, 9
Pennycuick, Dr. Colin, x
photographic equipment, 7; in Land Rover, 20, 22, 24, 141, 142; Image Intensifier, 146; telephoto lens, 158
photography; *see under* filming
Piaya, 61, 69
Predator Census, 114–15, 147, 148
Prince Philip, x

Index

Reedbuck, 153
rhinocerus, 80, 122
Rift Valley, ix
Run Cheetah Run (film), 96
Ruwenzori Mountains, Uganda, 8
   National Park (*late* Queen Elizabeth) 9

Safaris: **14–25**; fuel problems, 50–3, 66, 70–1; food 47, 50, 53; camping, 47, 52–3, 60; moving camp, 107, 114, 116, 117
Sale Plains, 39, 40
scientists, 114, 122–3
Scratching Rocks, 126, 141, 152
Seneto, 164; pack (dogs) 44–5; pride (lions) 136
Serengeti National Park, 9, 27, 47, 78–80, 97, 103, 106, 107, 147
   Research Institute, 40, 114, 123
Serengeti Had Not Died, (film) x
Seronera, 9, 37, 49, 51, 72, 74, 114–16, 144, 147
serval cats, 40, 97
Silali, 152
Simon, game guard to P., 116, 117, 119
spring hares, 63, 100
Survival Anglia Ltd., ix–xi, i, 26, 30, 46, 81, 90, 146, 167
Swahili, 58, 135

Tabora, 9
Tanzania, xi, 30, 36, 66, 109–11, 167; Central Bank 89; Tours, 70

Television, 1, 11, 26, 29; BBC-Time-Life, 96; Specials, cost of, 106; 130; *see also* Survival Anglia
tourists, ix, 7, 51; camps, 117; lodges, 121–2
trackers, 102, 104

Uganda, W. Railway, 8

Vehicles: Land Rovers, 17–25; 63, 70–1, 91, 98, 108–9, 113–14, 152–3, 159
   Range Rovers, 18–20, 47, 50, 53, 62–3, 66, 71, 91, 113, 117
   Toyotas (Japanese), 19
vultures, x, 57–9; Egyptian, 12–13; Griffon, 5, 39

Wachtsinger, Dr. 64, 68–9
Wakamba tribe, 102
warthogs, 115, 131, 146–8
wildebeest:
   herds of, 27, 36, 40, 52, 55, 58, 63, 81, 83, 87–9, 97, 100, 106, 122, 126–7, 146–7, 154–5, 163–4
   'kills', 10, 28, 59, 83–4, 86–7, 89, 131, 138–9, 141, 144–5, 156; and vehicles, 84–6; and zebra, 149–152
wildlife, x, 2, 7–8; predators & prey, 26–8; 31–4
Willock, Colin, xi, i, 30, 90, 167
Wings over the Rift (film) x

zebra, 10, 122; and wildebeest, 149–152, 153–4, 156, 157, 164

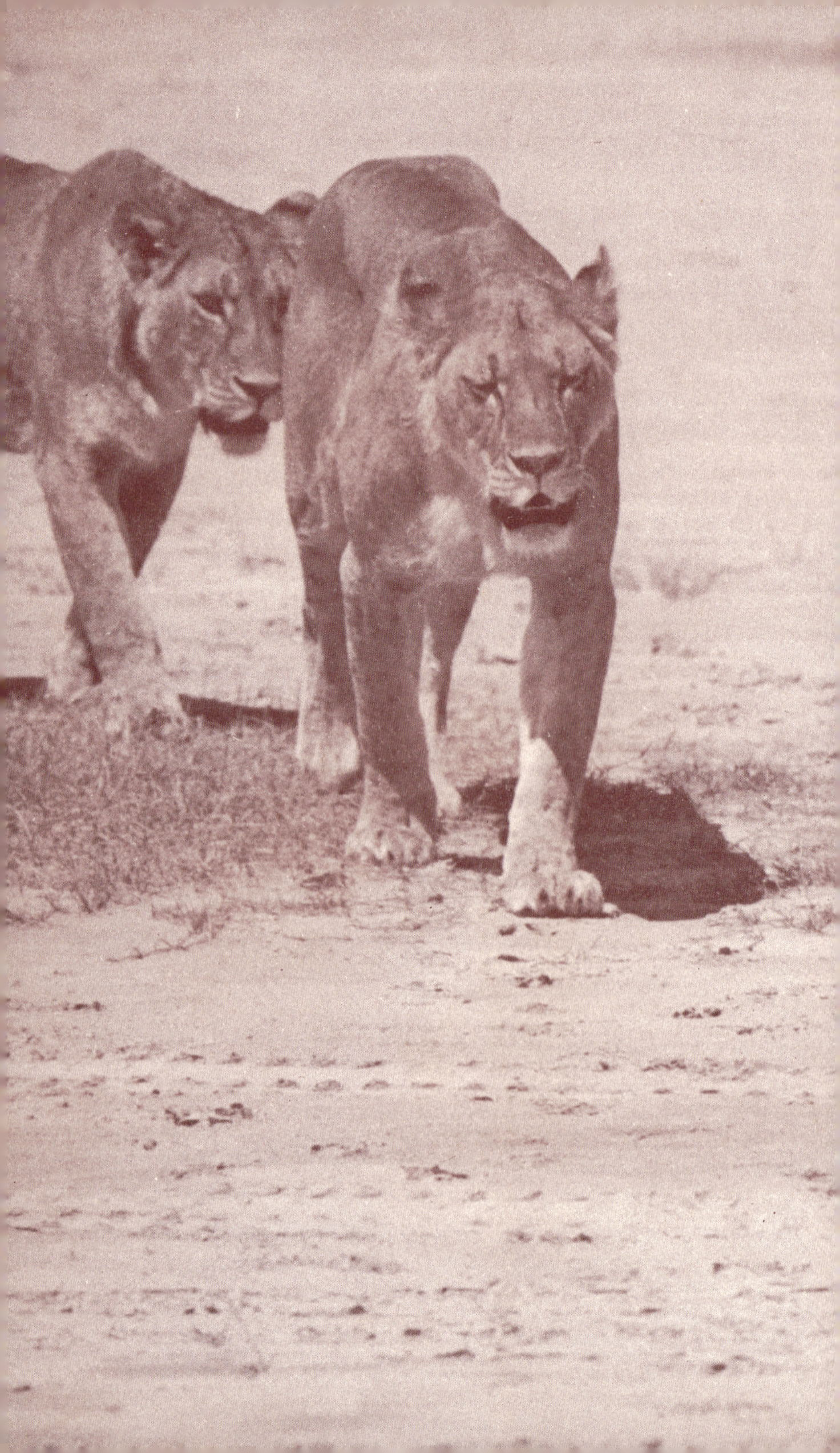